Also by Steve Langford:

Life in the Spirit

Reflecting on the Work of the Holy Spirit in Our Lives

Steve Langford

Order this book online at www.trafford.com
or email orders@trafford.com

Most Trafford titles are also available at major online book retailers.

The image used on the cover is an original work by Camille Harmon of Georgetown, TX.

Scripture quotations marked KJV are from the Holy Bible, King James Version
(Authorized Version). First published in 1611. Quoted from the KJV Classic
Reference Bible, Copyright © 1983 by The Zondervan Corporation

Scripture quotations marked "NIV" are taken from the Holy Bible, New
International Version®, NIV®, © 1973, 1978, 1984, by the International Bible
Society. Used by permission of Zondervan. All rights reserved. [Biblica]

Scripture quotations marked "NRSV" are taken from the New Revised Standard Version of the
Bible, © 1989, by the Division of Christian Education of the National Council of the Churches
of Christ in the United States of America. Used by permission. All rights reserved. [Website]

Print information available on the last page.

ISBN: 978-1-6987-1190-4 (sc)
ISBN: 978-1-6987-1189-8 (hc)
ISBN: 978-1-6987-1188-1 (e)

Library of Congress Control Number: 2022908343

Trafford rev. 05/04/2022

www.trafford.com
North America & international
toll-free: 844-688-6899 (USA & Canada)
fax: 812 355 4082

Contents

Introduction

Throughout the history of the Christian Church, the Spirit and the work of the Spirit have lived in the shadows of the life and ministry, death and resurrection of Jesus. Jesus, particularly his death and resurrection, has been center stage while the Spirit has been in the wings, in a supportive role. As a result, the average church member knows little of the Spirit's work, even though the Spirit is the means by which every one of us experiences God and the gift of salvation.[1]

A number of factors contribute to this pattern of overlooking the work of the Spirit. A primary reason lies in the nature of the Spirit's work. The Spirit's role is to point us to Jesus and draw us to God. Just as Jesus's work was to reveal the Father to us (John 1:18; 14:9), the Spirit's work is to be a witness to Jesus as a means of drawing us into a relationship with the Father.[2] The Spirit's role is an expression of the self-giving love and servant spirit that lie at the heart of the divine character. Living out of the same character as the Father and the Son, the Spirit is self-giving, not self-promoting. Following the Spirit's lead, we have focused on Jesus and his death and resurrection, paying little attention to the Spirit.

The scriptures also reflect this primary focus on Jesus. Whereas the four gospels relate the life and ministry of Jesus, there is no single book that focuses specifically on the Spirit and the work of the Spirit. In all of the New Testament, only four passages specifically speak of the Spirit and the Spirit's work in any detail. (See Chapter 1 below.)

Another factor in our neglect of the Spirit is fear. We humans commonly fear what we do not understand and cannot control. We seek to understand, explain, and define reality in our effort to have a sense of control over life, but the Spirit and the work of the Spirit lie outside our understanding and control, in the realm of mystery. Jesus used the wind to speak of the mysterious nature of the Spirit's work: "The wind blows where it chooses, and you hear the sound of it, but you do not know where it comes from or where it goes. So it is with everyone who is born of the Spirit" (John 3:8).[3] To embrace the Spirit is to surrender our need to understand, explain, and control. It is to embrace mystery.

As in every dimension of spiritual life, our ego is a factor in our neglect of the Spirit. Our ego-based identity is built on a twofold foundation of achievement and self-reliance. Our sense of self is tied to what we have accomplished, particularly in comparison to others. The motto by which we commonly live is expressed in the words of the preschooler who declared, "I can do it myself." Living in relationship with the Spirit calls for a spirit of glad dependence. As we live in relationship with the Spirit, we learn from the Spirit, we follow the Spirit's lead, and we look to the Spirit for power to do what we cannot do in our own strength. Such dependency goes against our ego's pattern of stubborn self-reliance.

The New Testament writers were clear about the Spirit and the Spirit's role in our salvation and God's eternal redemptive purpose.[4] In their minds, the work of the Spirit and the work of Jesus were inseparable. They were two parts of the same reality. What Jesus accomplished in his death and resurrection, the Spirit brings into reality in our lives. In Galatians 4:4–7, for example, the Apostle Paul spoke of God sending both the Son and the Spirit. The Son was sent to redeem us "so that we might receive adoption as children" (Galatians 4:5). The

Spirit was sent to nurture the spirit of adoption within us, whereby we cry "Abba! Father!" (Galatians 4:6; Romans 8:14–17). This spirit of adoption is a child's unquestioning trust in the Father's love. Such a spirit frees us from fear so that we live out of our identity as a beloved child of God and as an heir of the fullness of God. We live with freedom (Galatians 5:1, 13)—freedom from fear, from guilt and shame, from having to earn God's approval, from slavish obedience to the law. The biblical writers understood that the Spirit actively works to make God's salvation—the transformation of our hearts and minds, conforming us to the image of Jesus—a reality in our lives.

When we as individuals and churches overlook the work of the Spirit, we fail to experience what the Spirit seeks to accomplish in us and through us as the followers of Jesus. We live with little or no awareness of the Spirit's movement in our lives. We fail to recognize, much less respond to, what the Spirit is seeking to do in us. In short, we limit what the Spirit can do *in* us. We limit our spiritual growth and development. In addition, we limit what the Spirit can do *through* us. We limit how the Spirit can use us in ministry and witness to others in bringing the kingdom into reality on earth.

This book explores the role and work of the Spirit both in our individual lives (Chapters 2–24, 31) and in the life of the church (Chapters 25–30). These meditations draw on the New Testament writers' teachings about and references to the Spirit. While these teachings and references do not explain the mystery of the Spirit's work, they do give us glimpses of how the Spirit works. These glimpses position us to be more aware of the Spirit and more responsive to what the Spirit is doing.[5]

I offer these reflections with the prayer that understanding the role and work of the Spirit will help the reader be more open and responsive to the Spirit's work of

- drawing us to God,
- teaching us the ways of God that Jesus taught,
- transforming our hearts and minds into the likeness of Christ,
- nurturing within us an unfettered freedom in our relationship with God,
- teaching us to live out of a spirit of joy and peace and thanksgiving,
- guiding us in living the ways of God,
- empowering us to do what we cannot do in our own strength,
- gifting us with abilities to use in ministry to others, and
- leading us to love as Jesus loved.

May we learn to live in the power of the Spirit!

Chapter 1

The Scripture's Witness to the Work of the Spirit

I will pour out my Spirit on all flesh.

— Joel 2:28

These meditations on the Spirit's work are based upon the references to the Spirit and the Spirit's work found in the New Testament. The most concise teachings about the Spirit are found in four primary texts: the teachings of Jesus in John 14 and the writings of Paul in Romans 8:1–17, 26–27; 1 Corinthians 2:6–16; and Galatians 5:16–26.

In addition to these four texts, the book of Ephesians contains numerous references to the Spirit. It specifically identifies the Spirit's role in God's eternal, redemptive purpose (Ephesians 1:13–14). The book of Acts records the Spirit's work in the birth and expansion of the early church. Other New Testament writings make isolated references to the Spirit.

The Gospels

Each of the gospels speaks of the Spirit's role in Jesus's baptism and temptations as well as the beginning of his public ministry in Galilee. They record John the Baptizer's statement that the one who came after him would "baptize you with the Holy Spirit" (Matthew 3:11; Mark 1:8; Luke 3:16; John 1:33). Beyond these references to the Spirit in the beginning of Jesus's ministry, the gospels of Matthew and Luke note the Spirit's role in the birth of Jesus (Matthew 1:18, 20; Luke 1:35). The Spirit's influence runs throughout Luke's account of Jesus's birth (Luke 1:41—Elizabeth; 1:67—Zechariah; 2:25–26—Simeon). As they end, the gospels of Luke and John both speak of the Spirit as the means by which the ministry of Jesus would continue in and through the lives of his disciples. John's gospel ends with Jesus breathing on the disciples, giving them the Spirit (John 20:22). The gospel of Luke ends with instructions for the disciples to wait for the Spirit, who would clothe them "with power from on high" (Luke 24:49), setting up the book of Acts.

The Gospel of John

The gospel of John has more teachings about the Spirit than any other gospel. It records Jesus's teaching about being born of the Spirit (John 3:1–10). It also records Jesus's teaching about "rivers of living water" flowing out of the believer's heart (John 7:37–38), which the biblical writer identified as a reference to the Spirit (John 7:39). Jesus's most extensive teachings about the Spirit are found in what scholars call the Farewell Discourses (John 13–16).

In John 14, Jesus taught his disciples that he was going away—a reference to his death, resurrection, and ascension back into heaven. As a part of this teaching, he spoke of the coming of the Spirit. Although he was leaving them, he was not abandoning them (John 14:18). The Father would send the Spirit to live in them and among them (John 14:17; 16:7). Just as Jesus had walked with them, the Spirit would walk with them by dwelling in them.[6] The term Jesus used to speak of the Spirit captures the idea of one walking with them to help them. Jesus spoke of the Spirit as "one called alongside" (John 14:16).[7] This term has been variously translated as "Advocate," "Helper" (NRSV alternate reading), "Counselor," and "Comforter." Through the indwelling Spirit, Jesus and the Father would live in them (John 14:23). Unlike Jesus, who was leaving them, the Spirit would be with them forever (John 14:16). The Spirit would continue to do what Jesus had done. Just as Jesus had revealed the Father to them (John 14:7, 9) and taught them the ways of God, the Spirit—whom Jesus called the Spirit of truth (John 14:17)—would teach them, building on what Jesus had taught (John 14:26). The Spirit would lead them into even greater truth (John 16:12–15). In addition, the Spirit would empower them to do the things Jesus had done and to do even greater things (John 14:12). The Spirit would be like Jesus, doing what he had done and more.[8]

John's gospel records what, on the surface, appears to be a strange statement: "for as yet there was no Spirit because Jesus was not yet glorified" (John 7:39b). The gospel writer linked the gift of the Spirit to the resurrection and ascension of Jesus.[9] Jesus had to return to the Father before the Spirit would be given (John 16:7). The writer did not mean the Spirit did not exist. The Hebrew Scriptures clearly spoke of the Spirit and the Spirit's work. (See below.) I understand the writer to mean the Spirit had not yet been poured out on the disciples as on the day of Pentecost.

The Book of Acts

The book of Acts continues the story told in the gospel of Luke.[10] The promise of the Spirit recorded in Luke 24 is repeated in Acts 1 as Jesus prepared to ascend back to the Father. Jesus instructed his disciples to wait in Jerusalem for the fulfillment of what the Father had promised, i.e., the gift of the Spirit (Acts 1:4). They would be baptized with the Spirit (Acts 1:5) and filled with power (Acts 1:8) so that they could be witnesses of Jesus and the kingdom to every ethnic group in the world.

The promise was fulfilled on the day of Pentecost. As the disciples were gathered together in the Upper Room (Acts 1:12–14), the Spirit was poured out on each of them in the form of a tongue of fire (Acts 2:3). They were all filled with the Spirit (Acts 2:4), empowering them to speak the language of the foreign visitors who had come to Jerusalem for the festival of Pentecost (Acts 2:5–11). The biblical writer described the event using imagery from the Hebrew Scriptures—the rush of a violent wind (Acts 2:2), divided tongues, as of fire (Acts 2:3). In the Hebrew Scriptures, the presence of God is commonly associated with a storm (Exodus 19:16–18; Job 38:1; 40:6) and/or with fire (Exodus 3:2; 40:38). In using this imagery, the biblical writer was saying the presence of God descended upon them in the Spirit in the same way the presence of God descended upon the tabernacle in the wilderness (Exodus 40:34). That imagery suggests the disciples and the church were the new Temple, the dwelling place of God on earth (Ephesians 2:21–22).

Empowered by the Spirit, the disciples boldly bore witness to Jesus and the resurrection. Peter preached, interpreting the experience as the fulfillment of Joel's prophecy that the Spirit would be poured out on all flesh (Acts 2:14–21; Joel 2:28–32). Three thousand people responded to Peter's invitation to experience God's forgiveness and receive the gift of the Spirit (Acts 2:38–41). That response resulted in the birth of the church in Jerusalem. The church built their life around learning and living the ways of God that Jesus taught (Acts 2:42–47).

The Spirit played a major role throughout the book of Acts. The gift of the Spirit was the key indicator that individuals had become followers of Jesus (Acts 2:38; 8:14–17; 10:44–48; 11:15–18; 15:8; 19:2, 6). The Spirit empowered the early church to speak with boldness as opposition grew from the religious leaders in Jerusalem (Acts 4:31). One of the qualifications of the early leaders of the church in Jerusalem was that they be "full of the Spirit and wisdom" (Acts 6:3, 5; 11:24). The pairing of the Spirit with wisdom suggests the Spirit provided the wisdom the leaders needed to address the needs of the church. The Spirit is again paired with wisdom as Stephen taught in the Synagogue of the Freedmen (Acts 6:8–10). Stephen found comfort and assurance through the Spirit as he was being stoned to death (Acts 7:55). The Spirit directed Philip (Acts 8:29), Peter (Acts 4:8; 10:19; 11:12), Agabus (Acts 11:28; 21:10–11), Barnabas (Acts 11:22–26), and Paul with his entourage (Acts 13:4; 16:7; 20:22–23). The Spirit also provided guidance to the church at Antioch (Acts 13:1–3), the church in Jerusalem as they dealt with the issue of Gentiles in the church (Acts 15:28), and the disciples at Tyre (Acts 21:4).

The Apostle Paul

The Apostle Paul taught extensively about the work of the Spirit in the life of the believer (Romans 8:1–17, 26–27; 1 Corinthians 2:6–16; Galatians 5:16–26). His teachings echo the teachings of Jesus and reflect the experience of the Spirit recorded in Acts. We'll explore those teachings, along with other references to the Spirit by other authors, in the following chapters.

The Hebrew Scriptures

The New Testament understanding of the Spirit and the Spirit's work built upon and expanded the understanding of the Spirit presented in the Hebrew Scriptures. In the Hebrew

Scriptures, the Spirit is portrayed as being given to selected individuals, empowering them for the task to which they had been called.

The Spirit empowered those in leadership roles. The Spirit gave Bazalel the intelligence and ability to design and built the tabernacle in the wilderness (Exodus 31:3). Seventy elders were given the Spirit to assist Moses in leading the people of Israel in the wilderness (Numbers 11:17, 25–26). Joshua was filled with the Spirit when he was chosen to take Moses's place in leading the people (Numbers 27:15–18, Deuteronomy 34:9). The various judges were filled with the Spirit to empower them to provide leadership to the nation before they had a king: Othniel (Judges 3:10), Gideon (Judges 6:34), Jephthah (Judges 11:29), Samson (Judges 13:24–25; 14:6, 19; 15:14). As the kings of Israel, Saul (1 Samuel 10:6, 10; 11:6; 19:23–24) and David (1 Samuel 16:13; 2 Samuel 23:2) were anointed with the Spirit, as was Zerubbabel after the Exile (Haggai 1:14). The Spirit came upon Amasai, the leader of a coalition from the tribes of Benjamin and Judah, as he aligned with David when he was a fugitive running from Saul (1 Chronicles 12:18).

The prophets spoke of a coming king, a descendant of David, who would rule with justice and righteousness, bringing about lasting peace (Isaiah 9:6–7; 10:33–11:9; 61:1–4; 65:17–25). This coming king would be anointed with the Spirit. He was thus known as the anointed one—that is, the Messiah.[11]

The prophets who spoke for the LORD were also anointed with the Spirit: Balaam (Numbers 24:2); Elijah (1 Kings 18:12); Elisha (2 Kings 2:15); Zedekiah (1 Kings 22:24; 2 Chronicles 18:23); Azariah (2 Chronicles 15:1); Jahaziel (2 Chronicles 20:14); Zechariah, son of Jehoiada (2 Chronicles 24:20); Micah (Micah 3:8). The book of Ezekiel, recording the ministry and messages of the prophet Ezekiel to the people of Judah in Exile, is filled with references to the Spirit's work in his life (Ezekiel 3:12, 14, 24; 11:1, 5, 24; 37:1; 43:5).

The prophet Joel foresaw what the New Testament writers experienced.

Then afterwards
I will pour out my spirit on all flesh;
your sons and your daughters shall prophesy,
your old men shall dream dreams,
and your young men shall see visions.
Even on the male and female slaves,
in those days, I will pour out my spirit. (Joel 2:28–29)

Rather than being available to only select individuals, the Spirit would be poured out on all of God's people—male and female, young and old, enslaved and free. All would be empowered to do the work of God. When Peter interpreted the disciples' experience on Pentecost, he quoted this text from Joel (Acts 2:17–21). He said the gift of the Spirit was the fulfillment of this prophecy (Acts 2:16, 33). Peter went further to promise the Spirit to all who opened their lives to the truth of God's grace and forgiveness that Jesus proclaimed (Acts 2:38).

Chapter 2

Born of the Spirit

You must be born from above.

— John 3:7

"Born of the Spirit" is how Jesus spoke to Nicodemus of the work of the Spirit (John 3:5, 8).

Nicodemus was a member of the Pharisees, a religious teacher and respected leader. Recognizing that Jesus was "a teacher who has come from God" (John 3:2), he came to Jesus to talk about spiritual matters. Jesus told him that understanding spiritual matters, i.e., seeing the kingdom of God, required a new birth—being born from above (John 3:3). This new birth was the work of the Spirit (John 3:5–6). The Spirit's transforming work in one's life was what enabled that one to understand the ways of the kingdom and to participate in the kingdom. The Spirit's work opened up a whole new dimension of life—the spiritual dimension.[12]

Nicodemus misunderstood what Jesus said. He understood Jesus to mean a second physical birth. "How can anyone be born after having grown old? Can one enter a second time into the mother's womb and be born?" (John 3:4). Jesus was not referring to a physical birth. Rather, he spoke of a spiritual birth—being born from above through the work of the Spirit.[13]

Jesus spoke of two dimensions of life: the physical dimension and the spiritual dimension. "What is born of the flesh is flesh" (John 3:6a)—the physical dimension. "What is born of the Spirit is spirit" (John 3:6b)—the spiritual dimension. In our physical birth, we are born into the physical dimension and grow in our awareness of it. Similarly, the Spirit nurtures our awareness of and openness to the spiritual dimension. The Spirit leads us beyond our myopic focus on the physical dimension, opening our eyes to this other dimension of life. Through the Spirit's work, a whole new dimension of life opens up to us. The spiritual realm comes to life for us. The Spirit ushers us into this spiritual dimension. Through the work of the Spirit, we are born again spiritually—from above.

The Spirit's work is to draw us to God and into relationship with God. The Spirit enables us to experience God and to respond to God. The Spirit teaches us the ways of God and empowers us to live them. The Spirit is the means by which we participate in God's life as our own—what the gospel of John calls eternal life (John 3:15–16).

How the Spirit does all this lies in the realm of mystery. It is like the wind, Jesus said (John 3:8). We can feel the wind and hear it, but we cannot see it. We only see its impact. We can only know the Spirit's work by the results that are produced—awareness of God, openness to God, responsiveness to God, sensing the presence of God, understanding the ways of God, growing spiritually, a transformed life.

The Spirit leads us into life—life in the spiritual dimension, God's life, eternal life, abundant life (John 10:10). The Spirit is like "rivers of living water" (John 7:37–38). "Living waters" were spring water that flowed from an underground stream as opposed to water collected in a well.

Such springs provided a reliable, unending supply of fresh water in a desert region. The Spirit who resides in us (John 14:16–17) is an unending source of life for us—God's life, eternal life.[14]

Chapter 3

Pentecost: The Outpouring of the Spirit

All of them were filled with the Holy Spirit.

— Acts 2:4

In today's social media, individuals often share video clips with the admonition "Wait for it!" They are telling us something unexpected will happen. We will see it if we don't get impatient and move on. Just wait for it because …

As Jesus prepared to ascend back to the Father, he told his disciples, "Wait for it!" "Wait for the promise of the Father" (Acts 1:4).

For the disciples, Jesus's ascension (Acts 1:9) would have felt like losing him all over again. They believed they had lost him when they saw him die on the cross—but then came Easter Sunday! He was raised from the dead. They never dreamed they would see him again, but there he was, with them, very much alive. Once again, they enjoyed the gift of his presence on those special occasions when he appeared to them, but his ascension back to the Father brought those appearances to an end.

Telling them to wait, Jesus was telling the disciples his ascension was not the end of the story. There was more to come. God was still at work. And what God was going to do next would be just as unexpected as the resurrection. Through what God was going to do next, he would continue to be with them ... and not just on special occasions.

The outpouring of the Spirit on the Jewish feast of Pentecost (Acts 2:1–4) was the unexpected thing for which the disciples were told to wait. The gift of the Spirit was the continuation of the ministry of Jesus and the next stage in God's eternal redemptive purpose.

The outpouring of the Spirit was experienced as "the rush of a violent wind" and "as fire" (Acts 2:2–3). In the Hebrew Scriptures (the Old Testament), the presence of God was always associated with a storm and/or with fire. The LORD spoke to Job out of a whirlwind (Job 38:1; 40:6). God appeared to the people of Israel as a storm on Mt. Sinai (Exodus 19:16). The LORD spoke to Moses out of a burning bush (Exodus 3:2). God's presence in the tabernacle was symbolized in a cloud by day and a pillar of fire by night (Exodus 40:38). In describing the experience of wind and fire, the biblical writer was referring to the presence of God. Just as the presence of God filled the tabernacle once it was completed (Exodus 40:34–38), now the presence of God filled Jesus's disciples. Just as Jesus was "God-in-the-flesh" (John 1:14), now the Spirit of God filled each of the disciples and was in their midst. They were the continuing experience of God-in-the-flesh ... as are we! They were (and we are!) the "dwelling place for God" (Ephesians 2:22), a holy temple replacing the physical temple in Jerusalem (Ephesians 2:21). Through the empowering presence of the indwelling Spirit, God now dwells on earth in the lives of the followers of Jesus (us!).[15]

For the Hebrew people, the festival of Pentecost celebrated the giving of the law to Moses on Mt. Sinai. They viewed the law as God's supreme gift, telling them how to live. But, as Paul says, the law could not give them the power to do what was commanded (Romans 8:3). The outpouring of the Spirit at Pentecost became, alongside the gift of Jesus, God's supreme gift (Galatians 4:4–7). The Spirit took the place of the law. The Spirit teaches us the ways of God that Jesus taught (John 14:25–26). The Spirit teaches us the heart of God (1 Corinthians 2:12–13) so that we have "the mind of Christ" (1 Corinthians 2:16). In addition, the Spirit empowers us to live the ways of God (Romans 8:2–4; Galatians 5:16–18, 22–25).

Through the empowering presence of the indwelling Spirit, the disciples continued and extended the ministry of Jesus, proclaiming and establishing the kingdom. They did what Jesus did (John 14:12). They were God's partners in the kingdom ... as are we today! The next stage of God's external redemptive purpose was (is) the ministry of the Spirit indwelling and empowering God's people to bring the kingdom to completion "on earth, as it is in heaven" (Matthew 6:10).

Jesus instructed his disciples to wait—Wait for it! But with the outpouring of the Spirit, the time of waiting ended. The time for doing began—doing the work of God, continuing and expanding the ministry of Jesus, bringing the Kingdom into reality—through the empowering presence of the indwelling Spirit.

The Easter season leads us to and culminates in Pentecost. Pentecost—the outpouring of the Spirit—empowers us with the power that raised Jesus from the dead (Ephesians 1:19–20) so that we can live as God's partners, doing the kingdom work that Jesus did.[16]

May we experience this reality in our lives today! May it be the reality in *your* life!

Chapter 4

Live by the Spirit

Live by the Spirit.

— Galatians 5:16

T he story of Pentecost—the outpouring of God's Spirit—
ushered in a new stage in God's eternal redemptive
purpose. Peter, quoting the prophet Joel, described this new
stage as "the last days" (Acts 2:17). In this new stage, life as
we have known it gives way to that which is new. Peter,
again quoting Joel, used apocalyptic language to describe this
moving from, into. "The sun shall be turned to darkness and
the moon to blood" (Acts 2:19–20). This new stage in God's
eternal redemptive purpose centers in the presence and work
of the Spirit.

In this new stage, God—through the Spirit—now dwells
in (within) us individually and among us as a spiritual
community. Through the Spirit, we as a spiritual community
are the temple of God. We as individuals are the on-going
incarnation—the in-the-flesh embodiment—of God.

In this new stage, we are God's partners in what God
is doing in the world. God works through us—through
the empowering presence of the indwelling Spirit within
us—to accomplish God's eternal redemptive purpose. We

become—individually and as a spiritual community—the expression of the kingdom on earth, here and now. This new stage ushers in a different approach to living. To use the words of the Apostle Paul, we walk "according to the Spirit" (Romans 8:4). We live "in the Spirit" (Romans 8:9) and "by the Spirit" (Galatians 5:16).

Living in the Spirit stands in contrast to living according to the flesh (Romans 8:1–17; Galatians 5:16–26). The *flesh* was Paul's term for our default human nature. It refers to more than the physical desires of the body. It was Paul's shorthand term for the self-focused, self-serving spirit that is inherent to our human condition. It refers to our ego-centric nature that drives how we live and governs how we relate to others. This ego-centric nature leads us to unconsciously operate out of a self-indulgent, what's-in-it-for-me spirit. It is driven by deep-seated anxiety and fear that rob us of joy and peace. It creates conflict in our relationships, resulting in us–them, me-and-mine divisions.[17] The *flesh* refers to our old way of living. It is life as we have known it before the outpouring of the Spirit inaugurating the new stage of God's work.[18]

The way we typically deal with this default nature and the conflict it creates in relationships is through law. We create standards of behavior that tell us how to live. We adopt a list of dos and don'ts, moral codes of right and wrong by which we live … and by which we judge others!

Paul referred to this law-based way of living as "the law of sin and death" (Romans 8:2). This law-based way of living was and is inherently flawed. The law can only tell us what to do. It cannot give us the ability to do what it says. Consequently, we cannot live up to its demands. We cannot measure up to "the just requirement of the law" (Romans 8:4). No amount of self-effort—trying harder to do better—is enough. All the law can do is tell us how we should live and then point out how we failed, i.e., sin. At best, the law can only help us recognize sin (Romans 7:7–12).

In the new stage inaugurated at Pentecost, life in the Spirit takes the place of the law of sin and death (Romans 8:2). The Spirit empowers us to do what we cannot do in our own strength. The Spirit empowers us to move beyond our default, self-serving nature with its practices (Romans 8:13). The Spirit empowers us to love as Jesus loved (Galatians 5:22–23). The Spirit empowers us to live the ways of the kingdom so that the kingdom comes on earth as it is in heaven.

It seems to me many of us struggle to recognize, much less embrace, this new stage of God's venture and our role in it. Our old, default nature is still intact, even though the Spirit's work is to engrain the character of Christ in its place. We react out of our anxiety-driven, ego-centric nature rather than living out of the mind of Christ. We cling to rules and standards of right and wrong, using them to judge and condemn others as a way to avoid dealing with our own failures (Matthew 7:1–5), even though the Spirit sets us free from that way of living (Romans 8:2; Galatians 5:1, 13–15). We have not embraced the freedom that is ours or the grace in which we stand (Romans 5:1–2). We have not embraced our identity as the beloved children of God (Romans 8:15–17; Galatians 4:4–7) and the boldness it brings. We settle for the mediocrity of "the-best-I-can" rather than claiming the Spirit's power to do what we cannot do in our own strength.

The story of Pentecost, followed by Trinity Sunday, invites us again to life in the Spirit.[19] These two emphases call us to turn loose of the way things were and embrace the new, Spirit-centered stage of God's work—in us and through us. In us, the Spirit is at work to grow us up spiritually into the likeness of Christ. Through us, the Spirit empowers us to use our gifts (1 Corinthians 12:7) in an area of passion to make a difference in the life of another in the name of Jesus, bringing the kingdom into reality on earth as it is in heaven.

Trinity Sunday echoes the story of Pentecost. Paul's words capture its meaning: "Live by the Spirit" (Galatians 5:16).

Merciful God, may it be!

Chapter 5

Keep in Step with the Spirit

---

*Since we live by the Spirit, let us
keep in step with the Spirit.*

— Galatians 5:25 (NIV)[20]

As I grow older, I am aware that I struggle to keep up. Children often struggle to keep up with their parents as they walk hurriedly along. Their short legs have to work twice as fast to keep up with their parents' longer strides. As I grow older, I struggle to keep up with the work pace of others. My stamina is not what it once was.

It seems to me that those of us who are the followers of Jesus struggle to keep up with the Spirit. The Apostle Paul began his great text on life in the Spirit (Galatians 5:16–26) with the admonition "Live by the Spirit" (Galatians 5:16). He ended it with the admonition "Keep in step with the Spirit" (Galatians 5:25 NIV). His admonition "Live by the Spirit" was a call to embrace a new way of living.

We naturally live out of our anxiety-driven, self-indulgent default nature—what Paul called "the flesh." We seek to manage the inclinations of this default nature by adopting and conforming to some religious or societal standard of expectations—what Paul called "the law." Neither way empowers us to "love your neighbor as yourself"—what Paul identified as the whole law in a nutshell (Galatians 5:14). In fact, both these approaches to life end up in conflicted, broken relationships. This reality runs throughout Paul's thoughts on life in the Spirit. He began with it: "If, however, you bite and devour one another, take care that you are not consumed by one another" (Galatians 5:15), and he ended with it: "Let us not become conceited, competing against one another, envying one another" (Galatians 5:26). Conflicted, broken relationships dominate the works of the flesh he identified (Galatians 5:19–20).

Living by the Spirit, on the other hand, leads us to love as Jesus loved. "By contrast, the fruit of the Spirit is love" (Galatians 5:22). Love is the first of the nine traits Paul identified as the fruit of the Spirit. To be able to love as Jesus loved is the goal of the Spirit's work within us. The Spirit leads us and empowers us to be patient, kind, generous, faithful, and gentle—that is, to love as Jesus loved.[21]

Living by the Spirit involves responding to the Spirit's work in our lives. The Spirit teaches us the ways of God Jesus taught (John 14:25–26; 16:12–15). The Spirit teaches us the ways of grace and forgiveness, of seeing and embracing every person as a beloved child of God, of using power to serve. We cannot live God's ways until we know them. The Spirit teaches us God's ways.

The Spirit also guides us in living God's ways. The Spirit nudges us with the truth we know. The Spirit leads us beyond merit-based thinking that deals in deserving, calling us to relate out of grace and forgiveness. The Spirit confronts our us–them thinking that sees those who are different as "other," calling us to see and embrace them as a brother or sister (Acts 10:28, 34-35, 44–48). The Spirit challenges the what's-in-it-for-me orientation of our default nature, calling us to use our power to respond to the needs of others (Galatians 5:13–14).

The Spirit confronts those things within us that keep us from living the ways of God (Acts 10:9–16). The truth of God we know exposes what is in our hearts—our attitudes toward others, harbored anger and resentment, rigid, judgmental thinking, fear, etc. The Spirit works to cleanse our hearts, engraining the character of God within.

The Spirit empowers us to live the ways of God. The Spirit's work of teaching, guiding, and cleansing us culminates in the Spirit empowering us to do what we cannot do in our own strength. The Spirit empowers us to love as Jesus loved, to love those whom Jesus loved.

Understanding the Spirit's work, Paul's closing admonition was "Keep in step with the Spirit" (Galatians 5:25 NIV). His admonition highlights our role in this divine dance. We consciously choose to follow the Spirit's lead. We keep up with what the Spirit is teaching us. We keep up with where the Spirit is nudging us to put truth into practice. We keep up as the Spirit shines the light of God's truth on what is in our hearts. We keep up as the Spirit calls us to offer to God what is in our hearts so that God can cleanse and heal it. As we keep up with the Spirit, the Spirit empowers us to do what we cannot do in our own strength.

If we keep up with the Spirit, we will love as Jesus loved. We will love those whom Jesus loved.

Chapter 6

Led by the Spirit

---

*All who are led by the Spirit of
God are children of God.*

— Romans 8:14

In two of his letters, Paul spoke of life in the Spirit (Galatians 5:16–26, Romans 8:1–17). In both letters, he spoke of being led by the Spirit. Writing to the Romans, Paul wrote "all who are led by the Spirit of God are children of God" (Romans 8:14). Writing to the Galatians, Paul said, "If you are led by the Spirit, you are not subject to the law" (Galatians 5:18). He also spoke of being guided by the Spirit (Galatians 5:25).

What does it mean to be led by the Spirit? Chapter 5 identifies four things that are involved in being led by the Spirit:

(1) The Spirit teaches us spiritual truth—the nature of God along with the ways of God that Jesus taught.

(2) The Spirit nudges us with that spiritual truth, leading us to live God's ways of grace and forgiveness in specific situations and relationships.

(3) The Spirit confronts those things within our hearts that block our ability to live God's ways—attitudes,

harbored hurt and anger, the lack of a teachable spirit that manifests as rigid thinking, fear, our default what's-in-it-for-me self-serving nature, etc. The Spirit leads us to deal with these heart issues so that we might experience healing and spiritual growth.

(4) The Spirit empowers us to do what we cannot do in our own strength.

Notice the destination to which the Spirit leads us. The Spirit leads us to live the ways of God that Jesus taught. The Spirit leads us to love as Jesus loved. The Spirit leads us to love those whom Jesus loved. To get us there, the Spirit leads us on a journey of discovery, healing, and personal transformation. The Spirit leads us to God.

The Spirit's leading is evident in three primary areas of our lives: in our personal lives, in our relationships, and in our involvement in the world.

In our personal lives, the Spirit's leading is evident in how we think. Paul spoke of the renewing of the mind (Romans 12:2). The writer of Ephesians spoke of being made new in the spirit of the mind (Ephesians 4:23; also, see Colossians 3:10). Paul also spoke of putting on the mind of Christ (Philippians 2:5–11) and of having the mind of Christ (1 Corinthians 2:16) because we are taught by the Spirit (1 Corinthians 2:13). In this new way of thinking, the character of God and the ways of the kingdom begin to shape how we think. We set aside the ways of thinking we learned from the world—merit-based, if–then thinking; either–or, black-and-white thinking; us–them thinking, better than–less than thinking—and the old attitudes such thinking produced.[22]

This renewing of the mind leads to a transformed life (Romans 12:2). We learn a new way to live—God's way of grace and forgiveness. We live with freedom (Galatians 5:1, 13). We move beyond the shoulds and oughts of rules and laws. We move beyond guilt and shame as we claim and rest in God's grace and forgiveness (Romans 5:1–2). Peace and joy, coupled with a spirit of thanksgiving, become the inner disposition out of which we live (Galatians 5:22; Colossians 3:15). Old hurts and emotional wounds, along with the old shame-based messages that fueled them, are cleansed and healed. We begin to grow up emotionally–relationally–spiritually.[23] We learn to deal with and manage the anxiety that so often drives our lives. We become less emotionally reactive as we live with self-awareness and self-control (Galatians 5:23). We live as the children of God (Romans 8:14).

This personal, spiritual transformation changes how we relate to others. As we grow and change, our relationships change. As we grow up emotionally–relationally–spiritually, our relationships become healthier. Whatever is in our hearts—anxiety and fear or peace, anger and negativity or joy, harbored hurt and bitterness or thanksgiving—is expressed in how we relate to others. Whatever pain we have not dealt with gets dumped onto others in the form of anger, blame, criticalness, and judgment (Matthew 7:1–5). Paul said unaddressed and unresolved issues resulting in broken relationships is the normal pattern of our human condition (Galatians 5:19–20).

By contrast, the Spirit's leading is evident in our relationships, specifically in unity and oneness (Ephesians 4:1–3). Such unity comes through the ability to work through issues (Ephesians 4:15; Matthew 18:15–20) coupled with the willingness to put up with and forgive (Matthew 18:21–35; Ephesians 4:31–32; Colossians 3:13). A spirit of compassion, rooted in humility, governs how we treat others (Colossians 3:12).[24] We become more patient and kind, understanding and forgiving. Only a Spirit-transformed heart and mind makes such things possible.

The third dimension in which the Spirit's leading is evident is in how we live in the world. The Spirit leads us to invest ourselves in the lives of others to make a difference in Jesus's name. We use our Spirit-given gifts in an area of passion (1 Corinthians 12:7, 11) as our contribution to the Body of Christ (1 Corinthians 12:12–13)—that is, doing the work of Christ in the world. We live out of a spirit of generosity, giving freely of who we are and what we have for the good of others (2 Corinthians 9:6–12). We live out of a servant spirit, using our power in its many forms to address the needs of others (Mark 10:42–45; Philippians 2:5–11). We love as Jesus loved (Galatians 5:22; Colossians 3:14). We work to bring the kingdom into reality on earth (Matthew 6:10).

The Spirit is leading us and guiding us—on a journey of personal transformation and growth that results in our being able to love as Jesus loved. As many as are led by the Spirit will love as Jesus loved. They will love those Jesus loved.

Chapter 7

A Spirit of Adoption

You have received a spirit of adoption.

— Romans 8:15

The Spirit is God's silent partner in God's relationship with us. The Spirit actively works to make God's salvation—the transformation of our hearts and minds, conforming us to the image of Jesus—a reality in our lives.

One of the primary things the Spirit does in our lives is to change how we view and relate to God. The Spirit cultivates a spirit of adoption in our hearts. Paul spoke of this change of spirit in his letter to the Romans: "For you did not receive a spirit of slavery to fall back into fear, but you have received a spirit of adoption. When we cry, 'Abba, Father!' it is that very Spirit bearing witness with our spirit that we are children of God" (Romans 8:15–16).

The spirit of adoption is the spirit of a small child who, living with an unquestioned confidence in her parents' love, confidently calls out, "Daddy! Momma!" The spirit of adoption is a spirit of deep, unquestioning trust. It creates freedom and boldness in our relationship with God.[25] There is no hesitancy or fear in it. It is an inner attitude that leads us to run quickly to God for help, confident in God's love for us.

Living out of a spirit of adoption, we naturally turn to God with all that life brings us. The spirit of adoption is a spirit of glad dependency. Like children, we know God will provide and guide ... and we trust that provision and guidance. Such a spirit allows us to live as God's partners in what God is doing in the world. It transforms our relationship with God to one of mutual interdependency: God relying on us as God's partners, doing God's work while we rely on God for all we need to do that work.

The spirit of adoption is also a spirit filled with love for God. It is our love responding to God's love for us. It is the love of a child for her father and mother.

Deep, unquestioning trust, freedom and boldness, glad dependency, mutual interdependency, reciprocal love—such is the spirit of adoption ... and so much more!

The opposite of the spirit of adoption is a spirit of fear (Romans 8:15). Living out of fear, we hide from God as the man and the woman hid from the LORD God in the story of the garden (Genesis 3:8). Fearing judgment and condemnation, we don't want to be known or to be found out. We don't want to face how we failed to measure up. Fearing rejection and abandonment, we strive to do what we think is pleasing to God so God will accept us. Paul called this a spirit of slavery (Romans 8:15). If we were honest with ourselves, we would recognize that deep within, we fear God. We are afraid to be known by God. We are afraid to trust God. We don't want to be dependent on God. We naturally rely upon our own wisdom and understanding. Such is the story of the garden in Genesis 3 ... as well as the story of our lives.

A spirit of fear is based in merit-based thinking. It functions out of an earning–deserving mentality. Deep down, we believe we get what we deserve. A spirit of fear is tied to a deep awareness that we fail to measure up. No matter how good we are or what we accomplish, we know deep inside that we still fall short of expectations. We fail to measure up to what is expected. We expect to be judged, condemned, and punished for not being good enough.

In contrast to the spirit of fear, the spirit of adoption is grounded in grace. It is the settled assurance that God's love for us is unconditional. It flows out of who God is—God's character—rather than in response to who we are or what we do. The Spirit cultivates the spirit of adoption in our hearts by teaching us to rest in God's grace. We live by faith in the unconditional nature of God's love. "There is no fear in love, but perfect love casts out fear; for fear has to do with punishment, and whoever fears has not reached perfection in love" (1 John 4:18).

The Spirit cultivates within us a spirit of adoption. Everything else flows out of this foundational way of viewing and relating to God.

Chapter 8

Freedom From . . . To

Where the Spirit of the Lord is, there is freedom.
— 2 Corinthians 3:17

For freedom, Christ has set us free.
— Galatians 5:1

Life in the Spirit is a life of freedom. Christ died so that we might be set free. The Spirit cultivates this sense of freedom within. It is part of the spirit of adoption the Spirit cultivates within us (Chapter 7). Freedom is a natural product of God's grace. Having taught us to trust God's grace, the Spirit helps us rest in that grace. There, we experience freedom.

We experience freedom from what Paul referred to as the law. We are set free from the pressure of having to earn God's approval. We are set free from slavish obedience to the law in an effort to gain God's acceptance. We are set free from constantly striving to measure up. We are set free from our fear of messing up. We are set free from having to depend on our own self-effort. We are set free from having to defend and prop up our ego-based self. As we learn to trust God's grace, the Spirit moves us beyond such merit-based thinking and living.[26]

In addition, we experience freedom from the fear, guilt, and shame that are an inseparable part of merit-based, law-centered thinking and living. The Spirit leads us beyond the fear that is an inherent part of knowing we fell short and did not meet expectations. Reassuring us of God's grace and forgiveness, the Spirit quietens our fear of condemnation, judgment, and punishment (1 John 4:17–18). The Spirit soothes our guilt and heals our shame. The Spirit cultivates peace and joy deep within (Galatians 5:22).

Freedom from fear, guilt, and shame frees us to learn and grow. Our experiences of failure—which are a normal, inescapable part of our human condition—become opportunities to grow. Rather than obsessing on the failure (with fear, guilt, and shame), the Spirit gives us insight into what lies behind the failure. The Spirit reveals what is in the heart. This deeper understanding opens us to the Spirit's work of cleansing, healing, and transforming the heart. The result is a transformed heart and a change in our behavior. Cleansing the heart changes the behavior. This dimension of the Spirit's work is possible because we have been set free from fear, guilt, and shame.

Living in the power of the Spirit and under the guidance of the Spirit replaces this merit-based, law-centered way of thinking and living (Galatians 5:16–26). As we follow the Spirit's guidance and keep in step with the Spirit (Galatians 5:25), the Spirit will lead us to love as Jesus loved (Galatians 5:22). Rather than being a license to unrestrained self-indulgence, the freedom we experience through the Spirit becomes the pathway to fulfilling the law by loving our neighbor as ourselves (Galatians 5:13–14).

"For you were called to freedom, my brothers and sisters" (Galatians 5:13)—freedom to love as Jesus loves.

Chapter 9

The Mind of Christ

We have the mind of Christ.

— 1 Corinthians 2:16

The Spirit is the member of the Godhead who brings God's salvation—the transformation of our hearts and minds, conforming us to the image of the Son—into reality in our lives. The Apostle Paul identified the Spirit as the one who is transforming us "from one degree of glory to another" (2 Corinthians 3:18).

The Spirit's work has many dimensions to it. Chapters 7 and 8 present how the Spirit nurtures within us a spirit of intimacy, freedom, and boldness in our relationship with God. The Spirit teaches us to trust God's steadfast, faithful love (grace), thereby leading us beyond guilt and shame, beyond the fear of condemnation and judgment.

Another primary dimension of the Spirit's work is teaching us to think with "the mind of Christ" (1 Corinthians 2:16). As we grow in Christ, our thinking begins to be shaped by the character of God and the ways of God. The Spirit guides our thinking (1 Corinthians 2:13), moving us beyond the way the world taught us to think. The Spirit teaches us to be spiritually discerning (1 Corinthians 2:14). In short, we learn to think differently.

Paul spoke of this change in how we think as "the renewing of the mind" (Romans 12:2). He identified it as the key to being transformed. This same understanding is found in Ephesians 4:22–24 and Colossians 3:9b–11, where putting off the old self and putting on the new self happens by being "renewed in the spirit of your minds" (Ephesians 4:23).

Putting on the mind of Christ occurs as the Spirit teaches us the character of God and the ways of God (1 Corinthians 2:10, 12–14), along with the ways of the kingdom that Jesus taught and lived (John 14:26). These new understandings, in turn, confront the spirit and attitudes of our hearts. Through these confrontations, the Spirit works to cleanse the heart. "Create in me a clean heart, O God, and put a new and right spirit within me" (Psalms 51:10). The heart is cleansed as the mind is made new. Our hearts and minds are changed and our lives transformed through the work of the Spirit.

As the Spirit fashions the mind of Christ in us, we live out of the wisdom of God (1 Corinthians 2:7). We begin to relate out of grace and forgiveness, laying aside merit-based thinking. We learn to view and value, accept and embrace each person as a beloved child of God, moving beyond the us–them mentality of tribal thinking. We learn to value diversity as a gift from God, moving beyond the comparing and competing of better than–less than thinking. Secure in our identities as beloved children of God, we no longer seek to establish our identity at another's expense—"I'm not like them. I'm better than that." As we learn to live out of the mind of Christ, we use our power to serve others rather than to manipulate, control, or dominate others for our own advantage. All this kind of shifting from ... to is the work of the Spirit in our lives.

It all begins with the Spirit teaching us to think differently—from a spiritual perspective. Changing how we think leads to cleansing what is in our hearts. By changing our hearts and minds, the Spirit changes how we live. We are transformed by the renewing of the mind (Romans 12:2).

Chapter 10

A New Creation

---

*If anyone is in Christ, there is a new
creation: everything old has passed away.*

— 2 Corinthians 5:17–18a

The result of the Spirit's work in our hearts and minds is transformation. "All of us … are being transformed into the same image (the image of Christ) from one degree of glory to another; for this comes from the Lord, the Spirit" (2 Corinthians 3:18). Just as God created us in our mother's womb (Psalm 139:13), now the Spirit works to recreate us in the likeness of Christ. Through the Spirit's transforming work, we become a new creation. "If anyone is in Christ, there is a new creation: everything old has passed away; see, everything has become new! All this is from God who reconciled us to himself through Christ" (2 Corinthians 5:17–18a).

This transformation is a process—"from one degree of glory to another." We refer to this process of being transformed as growing spiritually. The Spirit works in the midst of life's experiences to help us grow spiritually. The transformation or growth occurs as we are led by the Spirit and keep in step with the Spirit (Galatians 5:16, 18, 25). The end result of this growth process is spiritual maturity. We are transformed into the likeness of Christ (Romans 8:29; Ephesians 4:3b). We become a new creation.

At the heart of this process of transformation and growth is the renewing of the mind. "Do not be conformed (literally: stop being conformed) to this world, but be transformed *by the renewing of your minds*" (Romans 12:2, emphasis added). The Spirit teaches us the things of God (1 Corinthians 2:6–16) and the things Jesus taught (John 14:26). Because the ways of God are different from our ways (Isaiah 55:8–9), the things the Spirit teaches us confront how we have been trained to think—merit-based thinking, us–them thinking, either-or thinking, black-and-white thinking, right-and-wrong thinking, ego-driven thinking. They call us to think with a different mind.[27] They call us to think with the mind of Christ.

The things the Spirit teaches do not just confront how we have been trained to think. They also confront what is in our hearts—the anxiety and fear that drive us, the attitudes that govern how we view and treat others, the self-serving, self-focused spirit out of which we live. As the Spirit transforms how we think—instilling the mind of Christ in us—the Spirit also works to transform our heart. The Spirit leads us beyond anxiety and fear into an ever-deepening trust in God's steadfast, faithful love. We move beyond our innate spirit of self-reliance into a spirit of glad dependency upon God. The Spirit cleanses the attitudes of our heart so that we see others the way God sees them. The Spirit nurtures a humble, teachable spirit within in place of the arrogance that views those who are different as less than and not deserving. The Spirit engrains a servant spirit that displaces our default self-serving, self-focused spirit. The Spirit cleanses our heart, transforming it. We become a new creation, transformed from the inside out.

As a new creation, our lives reflect the likeness of Christ. The old has passed away; everything becomes new

(2 Corinthians 5:17). Compassion and kindness displace the critical, judgmental spirit that is a natural part of our default nature. Humility and a teachable spirit displace the spirit of arrogance that fuels our critical, judgmental spirit. Patience and understanding displace the irritation and impatience we feel when people fail to measure up to our expectations or do things our way. We bear with others when we are at odds with them rather than attacking, discounting, and rejecting them. We are quick to forgive, refusing to hold onto a hurt or harbor a grudge. A spirit of thanksgiving and gratitude take the place of our fear-based scarcity thinking. Generosity takes the place of giving that is calculating, merit oriented, and governed by what-can-I-afford-to-give thinking. The peace of Christ displaces the anxiety that troubles our hearts and minds. Joy flows naturally from within. We live together in meaningful, supportive relationships that are patterned after the ways of God. We love as Jesus loved.[28] "All this is from God" (2 Corinthians 5:18a)—the work of the Spirit in our lives.

The Spirit is at work in us, recreating us in the likeness of Christ. The Spirit is at work transforming us, replacing the old with that which is new. The Spirit is at work growing us up, leading us to spiritual maturity. The Spirit is at work in us. As a result, we are a new creation.[29]

Chapter 11

The Pattern of Spiritual Formation

You have stripped off the old self with its
practices and have clothed yourselves with the
new self, which is being renewed in knowledge
according to the image of its creator.

— Colossians 3:9–10

There is no mystery to growing spiritually. Spiritual growth follows a simple pattern: from–into–by means of. We move *from* an old way *into* a new way *by means of* a catalyst.

We find this pattern described in the book of Ephesians: "You were taught to put away your former way of life, your old self, corrupt and deluded by its lusts, and to be renewed in the spirit of your minds, and to clothe yourselves with the new self, created according to the likeness of God in true righteousness and holiness" (Ephesians 4:22–24). Using the imagery of changing clothes, the writer spoke of putting away or taking off our former way of life–*from*–and putting on ("clothe yourselves") the new self–*into*.

Growing spiritually involves moving *from* an old way of thinking and living—"your former way of life" (Ephesians 4:22). This old way of thinking and living was how the world trained us to think and live. It was patterned after the ways of the world and lives out of the self-indulgent, what's-in-it-for-me spirit that permeates human interactions. Growing spiritually involves putting away—moving beyond—this old way of thinking and living.

Growing spiritually moves us *into* a new way of thinking and living. We put on a new self. This new self is shaped by the Spirit, patterned after the character of God and the ways of God. It reflects the servant spirit of Jesus.

The catalyst to this change is being "renewed in the spirit of your minds" (Ephesians 4:23). Putting off and putting on, moving from and moving into, happens *by means of* learning to think differently. The Spirit guides our thinking, teaching us God's wisdom (1 Corinthians 2:6–16). We learn to think with the mind of Christ (1 Corinthians 2:16). We are "transformed by the renewing of your minds" (Romans 12:2).

The Spirit orchestrates these experiences of spiritual growth. "All of us ... are being transformed ... from one degree of glory to another; for this comes from the Lord, the Spirit" (2 Corinthians 3:18). However, these growth experiences require our active cooperation with what the Spirit is doing. Progress requires us to consciously choose to embrace what the Spirit is doing in us.

We can derail these experiences of spiritual transformation at two different points.

The first critical point is when the Spirit seeks to teach us a new spiritual truth. A characteristic of our human nature is that we cling to that which is familiar and comfortable, resisting that which is new and different and unfamiliar. We use what we already think to judge any new concept. If it aligns with what we already think, we accept it as true. If it challenges what we believe, we reject it. When what the Spirit seeks to teach us challenges how we think and live, we naturally resist it and the change it requires.

The way we overcome this innate resistance is by embracing a teachable spirit that is willing to think, examine, and explore the "new" with which we are confronted rather than automatically rejecting it. If it is authentic spiritual truth, the Spirit will confirm it as aligning with the character of God and the spirit of Christ. That authentication calls us to embrace the new way of thinking as our own.

Embracing the new, Spirit-guided way of thinking brings us to the second critical point in the process. As we embrace the spiritual truth the Spirit has taught us, the attitudes of our heart— which govern how we view and treat others— are revealed. We are then faced with the choice of turning loose of our old attitudes, allowing the new understanding to shape our lives, or stubbornly clinging to them and remaining unchanged.

We see these two challenges in Peter's experience recorded in Acts 10. The Spirit taught Peter that he was not to call unclean what God had made clean (Acts 10:15, 28). Rather than immediately rejecting this new way of thinking—one that challenged what his religious culture had taught him— he was willing to explore it. The new understanding then challenged Peter's attitude toward the Gentiles. It called him to change how he viewed the Gentiles (Acts 10:34–35) and how he treated them (Acts 10:44–48). The new, Spirit-guided way of thinking led to embracing a different attitude—a cleansing of the heart. The transformed mind led to a cleansed heart. The transformed mind and cleansed heart resulted in a change in how Peter related to the Gentiles.

Peter moved *from* an old way of thinking about and treating Gentiles *into* a new way of thinking and relating to them *by means of* a new, Spirit-taught way of thinking. He put off a part of his old self—an attitude that his religious culture had taught him—and put on that which reflected the ways of Jesus.

This Spirit-designed, Spirit-orchestrated pattern is the means by which our lives are transformed into the likeness of Christ. It begins with the renewing of the mind—learning to think under the guidance of the Spirit and with the mind of Christ so that we live out of the wisdom of God (1 Corinthians 2:6–16).

Chapter 12

Growing Spiritually: How It Works

---

*All of us . . . are being transformed into the
same image from one degree of glory to another;
for this comes from the Lord, the Spirit.*

— 2 Corinthians 3:18

The biblical writers are clear—learning spiritual truth is the catalyst to spiritual growth (Romans 12:2, Ephesians 4:22–24, Colossians 3:9–11). Paul said we are transformed "by the renewing of the mind" (Romans 12:2). However, learning spiritual truth is only the spark that sets the process in motion.

Spiritual truth is about the mind—learning to think differently from how the world trained us to think—thinking shaped by the Spirit (1 Corinthians 2:7–13)—thinking that reflects the wisdom of God (1 Corinthians 2:7)—thinking with the mind of Christ (1 Corinthians 2:16). Such thinking is the starting point of spiritual growth.

For growth to occur—growth that produces not just a change of behavior but also a change of life—the heart must be transformed as well as the mind.

Here's how it works. Spiritual truth reveals what is in the heart. It reveals the attitudes we harbor along with the self-serving, what's-in-it-for-me spirit out of which we live. For example, my attitude toward my enemy is exposed when I embrace the truth that he too is created in the image of God and is one whom God loves.

Spiritual growth occurs when the heart is cleansed. The attitudes that govern how we view and treat others are changed. A servant spirit replaces the self-serving spirit. Our behavior changes when the heart is cleansed.

The cleansing of the heart is the work of the Spirit. We cannot change what is in our hearts. We can change our behavior—the external—but not what is in our hearts. We are dependent on the Spirit to change our attitudes and transform the spirit out of which we live.

While the cleansing of the heart is the work of the Spirit, we have a role to play in the process. Our role is to recognize what is in our heart (this recognition is the Spirit's work), acknowledge it to God, and invite the Spirit to transform it. That acknowledgment (confession) gives the Spirit permission to do the cleansing, healing work that is needed.

Our part calls for an intentional act of the will. We make a conscious choice to invite the Spirit to change what is in our heart. We choose to be different.

The challenge is we don't always want to change. We cling to harbored attitudes—not wanting to forgive one who has wronged us, not willing to change the way we look down on some group as "other," clinging to the sense that we are right and those who think differently are wrong, persisting in black-and-white, either–or thinking.

We cannot choose to change when we don't want to change. As a result, we stay stuck in old ways of thinking and living, unchanged from how the world taught us to think and live. We fail to grow spiritually. We wear the name of Christ without reflecting the spirit of Christ.

As long as this unwillingness to change persists—what scripture calls "a hardness of heart"—we remain stuck spiritually. We live in a condition of prolonged spiritual immaturity (Hebrews 4:11–14).

So how do we grow spiritually when we don't want to turn loose of these kinds of harbored attitudes? How can the Spirit change us when we don't want to change? The Spirit can cleanse this hardness of heart, freeing us to grow spiritually, when we are willing (1) to acknowledge that we don't want to let go of a particular attitude and (2) to pray "I want to want to." The Spirit who has the power to cleanse our hearts can help us "want to." The Spirit can change our hardness of heart.

Only when our hearts are cleansed will our behavior—and our lives—change.

Transformed Mind → Cleansed Heart → Changed Behavior = Spiritual Growth

→ Life Transformed into the Likeness of Christ

Chapter 13

How We Sabotage Our Own Spiritual Development

Do not despise the words of the prophets.

— 1 Thessalonians 5:20

Sadly, it seems, many of the opportunities we have to grow spiritually are sabotaged before they can bear fruit. They are sabotaged by a pattern that is inherent to our human nature. This pattern is reflected in the Apostle Paul's admonition to the Thessalonians: "Do not despise the words of the prophets" (1 Thessalonians 5:20).

The catalyst to spiritual growth is learning to think differently. We move from an old way of thinking and living (the old self) into a new way of thinking and living (the new self) by learning to think differently (Ephesians 4:22–24). We are transformed by "the renewing of the mind" (Romans 12:2). We learn to think with the wisdom of God (1 Corinthians 2:7) and the mind of Christ (1 Corinthians 2:16) under the guidance of the Spirit (1 Corinthians 2:10–13).

This catalyst is the work of the Spirit. The Spirit teaches us spiritual truth that confronts what we think and how we think. Prophets played a key role in this work of the Spirit. (In the New Testament, the term *prophet* was commonly used to refer to those who proclaimed God's truth—what we would today call preaching.) Thus, Paul urged the Thessalonians to not despise or reject what the prophets proclaimed.

This admonition brings us back to the pattern inherent to our human nature that sabotages our spiritual growth opportunities before they can bear fruit. We humans commonly reject those things that challenge how we think. We use what we believe to judge what we hear. If what we hear aligns with what we believe, we accept it. If it is different from what we believe, we reject it as false—not valid and not true. This pattern is so common that social scientists have given it a name: confirmation bias.

This common human inclination prevents us from hearing—much less accepting—the truth the Spirit seeks to teach us. It blocks the transformation process before it can begin. It sabotages the work of the Spirit.[30] The Apostle Paul seemed to understand this reality. In his exhortation to the Thessalonians, he wrote, "Do not quench the Spirit. Do not despise the words of prophets" (1 Thessalonians 5:19–20). We quench the Spirit—pour cold water on the Spirit's work—by rejecting the truth the Spirit is seeking to teach us through the prophets.

One of the characteristics of discipleship is a teachable spirit—an open mind that is willing to think and learn. The word *disciple* means "learner." As Jesus's disciples, we are students who are studying the ways of God Jesus taught—the ways of the kingdom—so they can shape how we think and live. One dimension of the Spirit's work is to teach us what Jesus taught (John 14:26).

Living with a teachable spirit does not mean we accept everything we hear. It means we are open—willing to think— yet discerning. Paul taught this in his exhortation to the Thessalonians: "Do not quench the Spirit. Do not despise the words of the prophets, but test everything" (1 Thessalonians 5:19–21).

Paul taught the Thessalonians to examine what they heard, that is, to be discerning. "Test everything." Was the character of God reflected in what they heard? Did it align with the life and teachings of Jesus? Was it an expression of grace and forgiveness or of merit-based thinking and living? Did it use power to serve or to control, to seek the other's spiritual growth and maturity or conformity to a moral standard or religious law? Did it view and value, accept and embrace all as beloved children of God, or was it an expression of us–them, better than–less than thinking and relating? Did it lead to the transformation of heart and mind (the interior realm) or focus on behavior (the external)?[31]

Having examined what the prophets proclaimed, they were to "hold fast to what is good; abstain from every form of evil" (1 Thessalonians 5:21–22). The truth they discerned was to determine how they lived … even when that truth called them to change what they thought and how they lived.

A teachable spirit, coupled with discernment, keeps us open to the Spirit. It makes us receptive to the Spirit's work. It keeps alive the opportunity for spiritual growth that the Spirit offers us through the renewing of the mind. It prevents us from sabotaging our own growth in Christ. It is the antidote to prolonged spiritual immaturity (Hebrews 5:11–13). A teachable spirit, coupled with discernment, is how we avoid quenching the Spirit by despising the words of the prophets.

Chapter 14

Stopping Short of the Destination

Let us go on toward perfection.

— Hebrews 6:1

It appears to be one of those throwaway verses of scripture—a seemingly insignificant detail recorded in the midst of far more important matters. "Terah took his son Abram and his grandson Lot son of Haran, and his daughter-in-law Sarai, his son Abram's wife, and they went out together from Ur of the Chaldeans to go into the land of Canaan; but when they came to Haran, they settled there" (Genesis 11:31).

Terah was the father of Abram—whom we know as Abraham, the one with whom God first made a covenant and the one to whom the Jewish people trace their origins. Our focus is immediately drawn to Abram because of his importance as our spiritual ancestor. Any reference to Terah is easily passed over. Terah lives in the shadow of his son Abram.

Yet, what the Hebrew Scriptures said about Terah catches my attention. Terah left his homeland of Chaldea (Babylon) to go to the land of Canaan—the land God promised to Abram, the land we refer to as the Promised Land. However, on the way to Canaan, Terah stopped in Haran and settled there.

Terah seemingly stopped short of his original destination. He didn't make it to Canaan.

As I read this historical note, questions immediately jump to my mind. Why did he settle in Haran? Did something happen that caused him to settle for Haran instead of Canaan? Did he set out for Canaan because the LORD had called him the way the LORD later called his son Abram (Genesis 12:1–3)? Was Terah the one with whom the LORD originally planned to enter into covenant? The text does not answer my questions. It only states the historical fact: Terah stopped short of his original destination, Canaan. The lack of answers to my questions leaves me to reflect on how we might do what Terah did—stop short on the spiritual journey.

Abram's call and journey to Canaan—like the wanderings of the Hebrew people in the wilderness after their deliverance from captivity in Egypt—are precursors to and metaphors of our spiritual journey. We, like Abram and like the Israelites in Egypt, have heard and responded to a call to live in a covenant relationship with the LORD. That call puts us on a spiritual journey toward a promised destination. For Abram and the Israelites, the tangible destination was the land of Canaan.

In popular theology, Canaan or the Promised Land is understood as a metaphor for heaven. In this kind of thinking, our destination is going to heaven when we die and thereby escaping hell. As common as this line of thinking is, it is not the biblical understanding. The New Testament writers identified spiritual maturity—being conformed to the likeness of Christ—as the destination of our spiritual journey.

The Spirit's work is to transform us into the likeness of Christ (Romans 8:29, 2 Corinthians 3:18). Thus, the Spirit actively works to grow us up spiritually. The Spirit initiates our growth by teaching us the things of God that Jesus taught (John 14:26). The Spirit teaches us to think with the mind of Christ and the wisdom of God (1 Corinthians 2:7–16). That new way of thinking leads to the transformation of our hearts and minds by the Spirit (Romans 12:2). The result is a Spirit-empowered change in how we live. The Spirit not only orchestrates our growth, the Spirit is also God's guarantee to us—God's pledge or earnest money—that we will reach our destination of Christ-like spiritual maturity (Ephesians 1:13–14). Before the Spirit's work is done, we will be like Christ (Ephesians 4:13).

This promise brings me back to Nahor who stopped short of his destination. Is it possible for us to stop short of the destination of Christ-like spiritual maturity to which God has called us? Is it possible for us to settle down somewhere short of what God wants for us?

The Hebrew Scriptures tell the story of the Israelites who stopped short of the destination to which the LORD had called them (Numbers 13–14; Psalm 95:7b–11). Eighteen months out of Egypt, the LORD sought to lead the people into the Land of Promise, but they were afraid of the inhabitants. They failed to trust the LORD to give them the land, rebelling against the LORD's command and refusing to try to take the land. As a result, they wandered in the wilderness for another thirty-eight and a half years until all of that generation had died. Their children and grandchildren were the ones who entered Canaan under Joshua's leadership.

The writer of the book of Hebrews used their experience as a warning about stopping short of the destination of spiritual maturity (Hebrews 3:7–19). He described his readers as being in a state of prolonged spiritual immaturity (Hebrews 5:11–14) and called them to go on to maturity (Hebrews 6:1).[32] He called them to build their lives around the spiritual truths they had been taught (Hebrews 10:19–25). He called them to be bold in taking their struggle to God, knowing that Jesus was a great high priest who could sympathize with them (Hebrews 4:14–16) because of the struggle and suffering he himself had endured (Hebrews 5:7–8).

The book of Hebrews clearly addresses the possibility of stopping short of the goal to which the LORD has called us. The author describes for us what it looks like to stop short.

We stop short of the destination when we stop growing spiritually ... when we resist the new way of thinking the Spirit is teaching us ... when we cling to old ways of thinking and living ... when we treat spiritual truth casually so that it no longer shapes our lives (Hebrews 2:1) ... when we no longer practice the spiritual disciplines that nurture growth (Hebrews 10:24–25) ... when we get comfortable with what we know, believing we are "right" ... when we, like Terah, settle for less than God desires for us.

Terah set out from Chaldea for Canaan, but when he got to Haran, he stopped. He didn't go on. He settled down. He stopped short of Canaan. As for us, "let us go on to maturity" (Hebrews 6:1). The Spirit is leading us to that destination.

Chapter 15

Loving as Jesus Loved

The fruit of the Spirit is love.

— Galatians 5:22

The Spirit's role is to make salvation—the transformation of our hearts and minds—into a reality in our lives. The Spirit teaches us to think with the mind of Christ (1 Corinthians 2:16b). The Spirit works to mature us into the likeness of Christ. The end result of the Spirit's work in our lives is to empower us to love as Jesus loved, to love those whom Jesus loved.

In his letter to the Galatians, the Apostle Paul identified love—God's kind of self-giving, agape love—as the first of nine traits he called the fruit of the Spirit. The ability to love as Jesus loved comes through the Spirit's work in our lives.

To free us to love as Jesus loved, the Spirit works to transform the spirit or inner disposition out of which we live. Inherent to our human condition is an inner disposition driven by anxiety and fear—fear of being hurt; fear of being left out, rejected, and abandoned; fear of being inadequate and not measuring up (i.e., being powerless); fear of being insignificant and unimportant (not valued or respected or loved). These fears naturally morph into an angry, negative spirit. The Spirit works to transform this inner disposition or spirit out of which we live. "The fruit of the Spirit is … joy and peace" (Galatians 5:22). The Spirit works to displace our anxiety and fear with peace, our negativity and anger with joy. The spirit or inner disposition out of which we live governs how we view and treat others. Consequently, what is in our hearts—the interior realm—is reflected in our relationships.

When we live out of an anxious, negative spirit, we are irritated with those who do not measure up to our expectations. We are critical and judgmental of them. Embedded in our criticism of them is an unconscious attitude of being better than them—arrogance. Looking down on them, we distance ourselves from them emotionally and physically. We are hard and harsh in how we think of them, speak of them, and treat them.

The joy and peace the Spirit cultivates in our hearts allows us to be patient rather than irritated, kind rather than critical and judgmental, generous in how we respond rather than feeling better than them, faithful rather than distancing ourselves, gentle rather than hard and harsh in how we think about, speak about, and treat them. "The fruit of the Spirit is … patience, kindness, generosity, faithfulness, gentleness" (Galatians 5:22–23). These five relational traits are what love looks like in our relationships.

We cannot love when we are anxious and afraid or when we are negative and angry. Joy and peace free us to love as Jesus loved. Thus, the key to loving as Jesus loved is being aware of and managing the inner disposition of our hearts— what Paul called self-control. "The fruit of the Spirit is … self-control" (Galatians 5:23). The Spirit makes us aware of the anxiety and fear, the anger and negativity deep inside (self-awareness). This awareness is a call to put ourselves in a position for the Spirit to work. It is a call to pray so the Spirit can transform what is in our hearts. The Spirit leads us beyond our anxiety and fear into peace, beyond our anger and negativity into joy. That Spirit-produced joy and peace free us to choose a different way of responding to the other. We choose to be patient, kind, generous, faithful, and gentle. Joy and peace free us to love as Jesus loved ... through the transforming, empowering work of the Spirit.

The Spirit works to transform our hearts and minds, empowering us to love as Jesus loved.[33]

Chapter 16

The Fruit of the Spirit
Is Joy and Peace

The fruit of the Spirit is love, joy, peace.

— Galatians 5:22

One of the nine traits the Apostle Paul identified as the fruit of the Spirit is peace—inner peace. Peace is what the Spirit produces in our lives as we walk in the Spirit (Galatians 5:16, 25), as we abide in Christ (John 15:1–11).

Both Jesus and Paul spoke of this inner peace. In John 14:27, Jesus said, "Peace I leave with you; my peace I give to you. I do not give to you as the world gives." In his letter to the Philippians, Paul spoke of "the peace of God which surpasses all understanding" (Philippians 4:7). Both spoke of the unusual nature of the peace that comes from God. Paul described it as a peace that cannot be understood or explained from a human perspective. Jesus described it as a different kind of peace from what the world gives.

The peace of Christ is an inner reality. It is something we experience deep within, at the core of our being. It is an inner quietness, a deep-seated sense of well-being and safeness the

Spirit creates deep within. Peace displaces the anxiety that is an inherent part of our human condition.

Anxiety is a nebulous feeling of unease or disease that lies just beneath the surface of our lives. Anxiety is the twitching of the old fears. It is the unconscious anticipation of something that will hurt us the way we were hurt in the past. Anxiety is the default state of our inner lives.

Peace, what Jesus called "my peace," is what quietens anxiety with its nebulous feeling of disease. It displaces the fear, stilling the inner turmoil and settling the inner restlessness. The peace of Christ sets us free from the power of anxiety, breaking its control over us. It sets us free from fear-based thinking and fear-based reactivity. It displaces our anxiety and fear ... in the midst of the very situation that spawned the fear in the first place!

Peace is not something we can manufacture or produce through self-effort. It is not something we can create or conjure up. It is what the Spirit produces in us. It is the result of the Spirit's work. While we cannot manufacture peace, we *can* place ourselves in a position for the Spirit to lead us into peace within.

The journey into peace begins with the *awareness* of the lack of peace. One would think that the recognition of this inner disease we call anxiety would be easy, but it is not. Anxiety and fear are our "normal" setting and thus outside of our awareness. They are also automatic reactions within us. They happen without our thinking and thus outside our awareness. We have to learn to be aware of our anxiety and recognize our fear.

The recognition of our anxiety and fear presents us with a choice. Do we continue to hold onto our fear (allowing it to hold onto us), or do we choose to move beyond it? Do we live out of our fear, or do we choose to let go of it? When we hold onto our fear, we give our fear control over us. It holds us in its grip. It shapes our thinking and governs what we do. Consequently, we react out of old patterns.

So the second step on the journey into peace is to *manage* the anxiety and fear. In John 14:27, where Jesus promised his peace, he said, "[D]o not let your hearts be troubled, and do not let them be afraid." In his letter to the Philippians, Paul exhorted them—"do not worry about anything" (Philippians 4:6). The original language in both texts carries the idea of "stop, do not continue." Fear and anxiety are a normal part of our human condition. Jesus's and Paul's words do not instruct us to *not* feel the anxiety and fear. Such is not possible. Rather, they call us to not dwell in our anxiety and fear. "Do not continue to live in your fear, with your fear, and out of your fear." They call us to move beyond our fear so that our fear does not dictate and control our lives.

Jesus and Paul called us to use our power to manage ourselves. Rather than attempting to control others or our situation, we manage what we are feeling along with the thinking that drives those feelings. We continue to live in fear and with fear only when we scare ourselves with our thinking.

We manage our anxiety and fear not by fighting them, not by resisting them, not by seeking to control them but by naming them. We acknowledge them to God. We pray. In doing so, we put ourselves in a position for the Spirit to displace our anxiety with peace, to create an inner quietness in the place of our inner turmoil.

Praying our fear is the third step on the journey that leads us into peace. The journey into peace follows the path of prayer. Through prayer, we remember, refocus, and reconnect with God so that we can rest in God's faithful love. Prayer is the way we manage our fears.

In his letter to the Philippians, Paul wrote, "Do not worry about anything, but in everything by prayer and supplication with thanksgiving, let your requests be made known to God" (Philippians 4:6). Paul didn't just say "don't worry."

He exhorted his readers to manage their anxiety and fear. "Don't continue to worry. You're doing it. Stop!" Then he told them how to move beyond the worry into peace. He instructed them to pray. Pray the fear. Acknowledge it. Express it. Bring your requests to God. In addition, Paul also instructed the Philippians in how to pray. They were to pray with thanksgiving. Thanksgiving is the key to moving beyond prayer driven by anxiety.

Thanksgiving is rooted in remembering. It is looking over our shoulder at the past, remembering God's faithfulness in past situations. Thanksgiving helps us remember God and God's faithfulness. It helps us remember how God was with us even when we couldn't recognize God's presence. It helps us remember how God strengthened and sustained us in the midst of our crisis. Thanksgiving helps us remember how God provided what we needed to deal with the crisis. It helps us remember how God transformed the experience, bringing good out of evil, life out of death. Thanksgiving helps us recognize how God blessed us and matured us as we walked a road we would rather not have walked. Praying with thanksgiving helps us remember. When we remember, we are in a position to reconnect with God.

Our fear and anxiety blind us to God. When we are living out of our anxiety and fear, our attention is on the situation. We are focused on the circumstances and on others and on what we are afraid might happen. In other words, our focus is not on God. In the midst of our anxiety and fear, the Spirit calls us to refocus on God and thereby to reconnect with God.

The Spirit guides us to remember so we can refocus. As we refocus on God, we can reconnect with God. When we reconnect with God, we can then rest in God.

Remember → Refocus → Reconnect → Rest

The Spirit leads us to rest in God's faithful love. Resting involves choosing to let go of our fear and our need to be in control. It involves choosing to trust. This Spirit-directed remembering, this Spirit-directed refocusing, this Spirit-directed reconnecting, this Spirit-empowered resting allows us to experience deep within the kind of peace that passes all human ability to understand or explain it.

This journey into peace is not some magic formula that automatically makes everything better. It is a process, a journey. It is a process of consciously shifting our focus from our situation to God, from frantically worrying about everything "out there" to managing what's "in here," from attempting to be in control to turning loose, from doing what we always do to resting. The journey into peace is choosing to trust God's faithful love. It is choosing to live in glad dependency upon the Spirit.

Peace is that inner quietness in the depth of our being that allows the joy of the Lord to flow in us and through us. Joy, like peace, is an inner reality we experience through the work of the Spirit. It is an inner disposition expressed in freedom, openness, and delight. Joy makes us open to God as we anticipate the goodness of God. It allows us to embrace all of life, even in the midst of difficult situations.

Joy is a condition of the heart. It is a dimension of the interior realm of one's life, an inner reality that flows from the depths of one's being. Because it is an inner reality, joy is independent of external circumstances. It is not dependent upon the events of our lives. The biblical witness is that joy can be experienced in the midst of life's stress, life's challenges, and life's pain.

Joy grows out of peace. As the Spirit leads us beyond the life-restricting power of anxiety and fear into peace, joy is free to flow from the depths of our being. We live out of an inner disposition of joy and peace. As we learn to live out of peace and joy, we can choose to love as Jesus loved.[34]

Chapter 17

Power to Do What I Cannot Do in My Own Strength

*You will receive power when the
Holy Spirit has come upon you.*

— Acts 1:8

P ower is associated with the gift of the Spirit. "You will receive power when the Holy Spirit has come upon you" (Acts 1:8). The Spirit provides the power we need to live the ways of God and to do the work of God.

The Spirit was poured out on Jesus at his baptism. Jesus began his ministry and completed his mission in the power of the Spirit. That same Spirit was poured out on the disciples on the day of Pentecost (Acts 2:1–4), just as Jesus had promised. The Spirit that empowered Jesus in his ministry empowered them and now empowers us as we seek to live the ways of God and do the work of God.[35]

Jesus's promise of the Spirit and the power the Spirit provides was made specifically in reference to bearing witness to all of the world about Jesus and the kingdom of God he put in place (Acts 1:8). The power available through the Spirit also applies to every aspect of the spiritual life. The Spirit empowers us to do what we cannot do in our own strength—from bearing witness to the love of God expressed in Jesus to doing any of the seemingly impossible teachings of Jesus to moving beyond the power of anxiety and worry to enduring the seemingly unbearable to breaking free of old patterns and addictions to forgiving the one who has wronged us to using our abilities to make a difference in the life of another in Jesus's name. The Spirit is our partner, the one who energizes every aspect of our spiritual lives.

The power the Spirit provides us is grounded in a spiritual principle—the Spirit's power is tied directly to our weakness.

The Apostle Paul learned this spiritual principle as he wrestled with his thorn in the flesh (2 Corinthians 12:7). Paul pleaded with God to remove this unidentified issue that created such a struggle for him. God's answer to Paul's prayer was "My grace is sufficient for you, for (my) power is made perfect in weakness" (2 Corinthians 12:9).

There are two parts to God's answer to Paul's prayer. The first was the assurance that God's grace would sustain Paul in his struggle. He would not be overcome or defeated by it. He would be victorious *through what God provided*! The second part of God's answer states the underlying principle to this word of assurance: God's power only comes into play when our power fails—in our weakness! God's power is "made perfect"—the idea is "doing what it was intended to do"—as the Spirit empowers us to do what we cannot do in our own strength.

This spiritual principle rubs us the wrong way. We don't like to be weak. Being weak implies we are inadequate. It means we are dependent. We want to be self-sufficient and independent—or at least, we want to believe we are. We are like the young child who tells her mother, "I can do it myself!" However, as long as we rely upon our own wisdom and strength, we will never know the power the Spirit provides. We will never fully live the ways of God that Jesus taught or do the work of God we have been called to do as God's partners in the world.

The Apostle Paul learned this great principle and built his life upon it. "So I will boast all the more gladly of my weaknesses, so that the power of Christ may dwell in me. For whenever I am weak, then I am strong" (2 Corinthians 12:9–10). Paul learned to live out of a spirit of glad dependency on God, trusting God to help him do what he could not do in his own strength. The spirit of glad dependency allowed the power of Christ—the power of the Spirit—to live in him.[36]

So how do we access this power of the Spirit? We do what Paul did: we pray. We pray our struggle. Rather than giving up in frustration and defeat, we acknowledge to God (confess) what we cannot do. We stay engaged in the struggle, giving God permission to work in it. We wait for God's response— the grace that is adequate, the guidance and insight the Spirit gives, the power to do what we cannot do in our own strength.

What might we be able to do—in living the ways of God that Jesus taught, in doing the work of God in the world—if we trusted the Spirit to empower us to do what we cannot do in our own strength? What might that look like for you?

What struggle is the Spirit leading us to pray?

Chapter 18

Power to Be a Witness

You will be my witnesses.

— Acts 1:8

The promise of the Spirit's power was specifically tied to the call to be a witness of Jesus and the kingdom he proclaimed. "You will receive power when the Holy Spirit has come upon you; and you will be my witnesses in Jerusalem, in all Judea and Samaria, and to the ends of the earth" (Acts 1:8). The Spirit empowers us to be witnesses of Jesus and the kingdom. Yet few things stir fear in the heart of most church members as this expectation that we are to be witnesses. Most of us are afraid to speak about our faith or our relationships with God in Christ.

A number of factors contribute to this fear. We feel inadequate and unqualified. We don't believe we have anything of significance to share—no Damascus road experience like Paul. We unconsciously recognize the gap between what we profess and our own lives. We don't want to come across as being arrogant, "holier than thou," or judgmental. We are afraid of how the other will react or what the other will think of us. We feel vulnerable, exposed—open to ridicule or challenge. We are afraid of losing face.

Not knowing how to deal with our fear, we come up with substitutes to actually having to talk about our spiritual lives. We want to believe our lives are our witness, specifically our involvement in the life of the institutional church. We want to believe the morals by which we live or the acts of charity we perform will speak for us. If we do dare to speak, it is to invite someone to attend our church or a special event the church is hosting.

Misunderstandings about being a witness—coupled with awkward, embarrassing experiences—fuel our fear. We commonly associate being a witness with trying to convince another to believe a certain thing that involves telling them how sinful they are. We think of witness in terms of confronting complete strangers or feeling obligated to "witness" to everyone everywhere. We think of witness as telling someone how to go to heaven when they die. Both our fears and our misunderstandings ignore the Spirit's role in our being witnesses. The Spirit empowers us to be witnesses.

There are at least two dimensions to being a witness—both are the work of the Spirit.

The first part of being a witness is experiencing the grace of God and the transforming work of the Spirit. We have to have something of our own to share. Our experience of God and God's work in our lives is far more than being involved in the life of an institutional church or being moral or doing acts of charity. None of these things are particularly unique.

The Spirit's work in our lives is transformative. It moves us beyond what we once were into something new that can only be explained as the work of God in our lives—from guilt and shame into forgiveness, from trying hard to gain God's approval into freedom, from hesitancy with God into boldness, from anxiety and worry into peace and joy, from us–them thinking into seeing and embracing all as beloved children of God, from judging another with the subtle arrogance of "being better than" into understanding and compassion.

The new the Spirit creates in our lives sets us apart, makes us different. It puts us out of step with the society in which we live. That difference calls for an explanation.

The second part of being a witness is offering an explanation for how we are different. It is telling our story. It is sharing our experience of God.[37]

The Spirit empowers us to tell our story. The book of Acts is full of stories of the early followers of Jesus telling of their experience, in the power of the Spirit. "Filled with the Spirit" or "full of the Spirit" was a factor in their sharing.[38] Filled with the Holy Spirit, the first disciples bore witness to Jesus on the Day of Pentecost (Acts 2:4). Peter, filled with the Holy Spirit, answered the accusations of the Sanhedrin when he was arrested (Acts 4:8). He offered his defense in the power of the Spirit. "We are witnesses to these things, and so is the Holy Spirit, whom God has given to those who obey him" (Acts 5:32).

Peter's statement reminds us that the Spirit is bearing witness to Jesus and the kingdom. It is part of the Spirit's work. The Spirit empowers us to do what the Spirit does—bear witness to Jesus and the ways of God Jesus taught. The Spirit bears witness through our witness. The Spirit uses our witness to draw others to God and into a relationship with God.

One particular story in the book of Acts teaches us how to deal with the fear that is a normal part of our experience. In the face of growing opposition and the threat of persecution, the early followers were afraid—including Peter and John, the leaders of that early church (Acts 4:23). They dealt with their fear by praying. They took their fear to God (Acts 4:24–30). As a result, they were all filled with the Spirit and spoke the word boldly (Acts 4:31). Boldness is not the absence of fear. It is the courage to act in the face of fear. Boldness came as they confessed their fear to God. The Spirit empowered them to speak in spite of their fear. In their weakness, they experienced God's power through the filling of the Spirit.

Being a witness is not attempting to convince someone to believe what we believe. It is simply telling our story. It is sharing our experience of God and the difference that experience made in our lives. It is as simple as telling what we were like before the experience, relating the experience, and identifying how we are different because of the experience.[39]

The Spirit empowers us to be witnesses. The Spirit works to transform our hearts and minds, giving us something to share. The Spirit empowers us to share it. The Spirit provides the opportunity to share it. The Spirit helps us recognize the opportunity, guiding us in what and how to share. The Spirit empowers us as we share it.

Being a witness is telling our story—in the power of the Spirit, under the guidance of the Spirit, in partnership with the Spirit.

Chapter 19

Filled with the Spirit

Be filled with the Spirit.

— Ephesians 5:18b

It is one in a long series of exhortations about living as a follower of Jesus—live in love, live as children of light, live as those who are wise (Ephesians 5:2, 8, 15). In the face of a barrage of exhortations (the writer of Ephesians was not the only preacher to get carried away with telling others how to live), it is easy to tune out the specifics of the exhortations. After all, such barrages can be overwhelming, the expectations seemingly impossible to measure up to. They often stir feelings of failure and inadequacy, leading us to settle for the mediocrity of "as best I can." This particular exhortation, however, has to do with the Spirit: "Be filled with the Spirit" (Ephesians 5:18).

What did the biblical writer mean by "Be filled with the Spirit"? The exhortation falls under the category of living as those who are wise (Ephesians 5:15–21). In this section, the writer calls us to live as those who "understand what the will of the Lord is" (Ephesians 5:17). He defines being wise as knowing the ways of God—the way of self-giving, servant love, the way of grace and forgiveness, etc.—and allowing that knowledge to shape how we live in the specific relationships and situations of our lives, i.e., the will of God. That's when the exhortation about the Spirit comes in—"Be filled with the Spirit." The context helps us understand the writer's meaning.

The Spirit is the one who teaches us the ways of God and who guides us in how to live those ways in our own lives. Thus, to be filled with the Spirit is to allow the Spirit to guide us in living the ways of God in our relationships. It is to live under the influence of the Spirit. This "under the influence" meaning is reinforced by the fuller exhortation "Do not get drunk with wine, for that is debauchery; but be filled with the Spirit." When we are drunk, we are under the influence of alcohol. The alcohol affects what we say and do. To be filled with the Spirit is to allow the Spirit to shape what we say and do. Being under the influence of the Spirit means we will live the ways of God—the way of self-giving, servant love, the way of grace and forgiveness, etc. To use the words of Ephesians, we will "be subject to one another out of reverence for Christ" (Ephesians 5:21). We will live out of a servant spirit, giving ourselves for the good of the other.

Some teach that to be filled with the Spirit is to be able to speak in tongues (1 Corinthians 12:10, 14:4–19)—a special prayer language. For them, speaking in tongues is evidence that one is under the influence of the Spirit. This understanding of what it means to be filled with the Spirit overlooks the Spirit's primary work: to transform our hearts and minds, conforming us to the likeness of Christ, so that we love as Jesus loved and love those Jesus loved. A servant spirit, reflected in the ability to love as Jesus loved, is the real indicator that we are filled with the Spirit, not the gift of a special prayer language.

The exhortation to be filled with the Spirit raises a second question: how? How are we filled with the Spirit? Being filled with the Spirit is not something we do. It is something that is done to us. Note the verb is passive—"be filled." We are the recipients of the filling. The Spirit is the one doing the action. The Spirit fills us. We cannot command or orchestrate or manipulate the Spirit into filling us. We can only receive the Spirit's work.

What we can do is place ourselves in a position to receive. We can place ourselves in a position for the Spirit to fill us. We do so by cultivating an attitude of openness to the Spirit. We seek to be aware of the Spirit and the Spirit's movement in our hearts and minds. We pay attention to the interior realm where the Spirit lives and works. In addition, we embrace a spirit of glad dependency upon the Spirit. Knowing that in our own strength, we cannot love as Jesus loves, we turn to the Spirit for guidance in how to love as Jesus loved as well as for the strength to do so. As we saw in the previous chapter, we place ourselves in a position to be filled with the Spirit by praying our struggle and fears—especially within a spiritual community. The early disciples confessed their fear to one another and to God (Acts 4:23–31). Confessing and then praying our struggle and fears puts us in a position to be filled with the Spirit.

These two attitudes—openness to the Spirit and a spirit of glad dependency—are cultivated through the spiritual practice of meditation. In addition, the author of Ephesians points to the importance of worship and spiritual community in cultivating these attitudes. The writer linked being filled with the Spirit with "psalms and hymns and spiritual songs" sung together out of a spirit of thanksgiving in a spiritual community (Ephesians 5:19–20).

The writer of Ephesians reminds us that to be a follower of Jesus is to embrace a different way of life, one shaped by and patterned after the ways of God. We are to live as beloved children who live in love, imitating God (Ephesians 5:1–2), as children of light who forsake the ways of darkness (Ephesians 5:8), as those who are wise because they understand the will of the Lord (Ephesians 5:15). The writer also reminds us that the Spirit is the key to living this God-shaped way of life. The Spirit teaches us the ways of God, guides us in how to live them in the specifics of our lives, and empowers us to do what we cannot do in our own strength.

If we are to live the ways of God, we must be filled with the Spirit. We must learn to live under the influence of the Spirit.

Chapter 20

The Spirit's Role in Prayer

Pray in the Spirit.

— Ephesians 6:18

It's one of those statements—actually an exhortation, a command—that is easily overlooked. It comes at the end of the letter, after the main theme had been laid to rest and the author was bringing his letter to a close. It's one of those last comments that we often overlook. In fact, we generally skip over it. Yet, when we reflect on it, we find it to be full of wisdom that can enrich our spiritual lives. It teaches us how to pray.

"Pray in the Spirit" (Ephesians 6:18). Some understand praying in the Spirit to refer to the phenomenon known as speaking in tongues—a prayer language some people experience. However, this exhortation suggests there is more to praying in the Spirit than speaking in tongues. This exhortation teaches us that the Spirit plays a vital role in our praying.

The Spirit prompts us to pray, stirring our sense of need to pray as well as our desire to pray.[40] The Spirit assures us that God accepts us unconditionally, freeing us from being hesitant or timid about coming to God in prayer (Romans

8:14–16). The Spirit cultivates the confidence to pray boldly (Hebrews 4:14–16), teaching us to trust God's delight in giving and generosity in doing so.

"Pray in the Spirit" calls us to allow the Spirit to guide our prayer. In his letter to the church at Corinth, Paul said the Spirit searches "the depths of God" (1 Corinthians 2:10). The Spirit knows the heart and mind of God. Thus, the Spirit knows "what is truly God's" (1 Corinthians 2:11). The Spirit's role is to lead us to know God and the ways of God (1 Corinthians 2:12). The Spirit guides us in connecting with God. The Spirit helps us align our prayers with the will of God.[41]

When we do not consciously involve the Spirit in our praying, our prayers tend to become monologues. We are like the person who talks nonstop, moving from one topic or story to the next, seemingly not even stopping to take a breath. These people dominate every conversation. In doing so, they control the relationship and keep the focus on themselves. Without the Spirit, we do all the talking when we pray. We control the relationship. We keep the focus on ourselves. Our prayers tend to be little more than reciting the grocery list of things we want God to do. Without the Spirit, our prayers become something we do—a task—rather than a relationship we enjoy. They become just another item on our to-do list.

"Pray in the Spirit" calls us to consciously and intentionally involve the Spirit when we pray. What does that look like? We begin by stilling our hearts and minds. "Be still and know that I am God" (Psalms 46:10). We do not rush into prayer. We center ourselves so that we can focus on connecting with God. I use controlled, slow, deep breathing to help me become still. Then we ask the Spirit to guide our thoughts as we pray. As we sit in stillness, we pay attention to where our thoughts go, seeking to understand what the Spirit wants us to see. We are making space for God to speak. We are listening to what God says through the Spirit. When we share our petitions and concerns, we take time to be still afterward, seeking to discern the Spirit's guidance. Even after our prayer time is "over," we continue to be attuned to what the Spirit brings to mind. Prayer becomes a dialogue that continues through the day.

Prayer is not one of the things we generally associate with the Spirit, but the Spirit guides us into deep, meaningful connection—and conversation!—with God.

Chapter 21

The Spirit Intercedes

The Spirit intercedes for the saints
according to the will of God.

— Romans 8:27

T he Spirit plays a larger role in prayer than most of us know.
According to the Apostle Paul, the Spirit actually prays
for us.

> Likewise, the Spirit helps us in our weakness; for
> we do not know how to pray as we ought, but
> that very Spirit intercedes with sighs too deep
> for words. And God, who searches the heart,
> knows what is the mind of the Spirit because the
> Spirit intercedes for the saints according to the
> will of God. (Romans 8:26–27)

The Spirit helps us pray, particularly during those difficult
times when we have difficulty praying. Times of suffering[42]
can be overwhelming and consuming. We get caught up in
our pain—both our physical pain and our emotional pain—
seemingly unable to escape their power. During such times,
it is difficult to pray. Our prayer is more of a cry of pain

than a consciously formed prayer. We don't know for what to pray other than for relief from the pain. "We don't know how to pray as we ought" (Romans 8:26). Paul refers to such experiences as "our weakness."

When we don't know how to pray or for what to pray, the Spirit prays for us. The Spirit intercedes on our behalf. The Spirit prays the prayer we don't know how to pray. "That very Spirit intercedes with sighs too deep for words" (Romans 8:26). The Spirit intercedes for what we need. The Spirit intercedes "according to the will of God" (Romans 8:27).

God's will is to transform our experience of suffering into a means of spiritual growth—what Paul called "for good" (Romans 8:28). God's desire is for us to "be conformed to the image of his Son" (Romans 8:29). A primary means by which God matures us spiritually is by transforming our painful experiences.

We have a role to play in the transformation of our suffering. Our response to our suffering is a determining factor in how God can work in it and what God can bring out of it. That is where the Spirit's intercession comes in. The Spirit intercedes for us. The Spirit prays for what we need to deal with our suffering in a way that allows God to transform it into spiritual growth. The Spirit intercedes for us so that we can be receptive to how God will work in the painful experience.

The Spirit intercedes for us. The Spirit prays for us when we cannot pray ourselves. The Spirit prays for what we need.

Chapter 22

The Sword of the Spirit

Take the sword of the Spirit,
which is the word of God.

— Ephesians 6:17

A sword is not something we normally associate with the Spirit, but the writer of Ephesians spoke of the sword of the Spirit (Ephesians 6:17). It was listed as a part of the armor of God.

The writer exhorted his readers to stand firm in the face of a hostile world. They had once followed the ways of the world (Ephesians 2:1–2) but now, as the followers of Jesus, they were living as the children of God (Ephesians 5:1), following God's way of self-giving love (Ephesians 5:2), living out of a servant spirit (Ephesians 5:21). They were putting off their old selves, which followed the self-indulgent ways of the world, and were putting on new selves that reflected the likeness of Christ (Ephesians 4:22–24). Now they had to stand firm against the pressures of world.

The world in which they lived—and in which we live!— was hostile to the ways of God. The author of Ephesians attributed this hostility to spiritual forces of evil aligned against God and the ways of God. He spoke of "the course of this world" as "following the ruler of the power of the air" (Ephesians 2:1–2). Consequently, we humans live out of a spirit of disobedience (Ephesians 2:2). He spoke of "the wiles of the devil" (Ephesians 6:10) and of "cosmic powers of this present darkness" and of "spiritual forces of evil in the heavenly places" (Ephesians 6:12).

Because the Ephesians 6 text speaks of the devil along with cosmic powers and spiritual forces of evil (Ephesians 6:12), some interpreters use this text to speak of spiritual warfare. They understand our struggle as the followers of Jesus to be a struggle with Satan. I understand our challenge to be a hostile world that embodies the ways of evil rather than following the ways of God (Ephesians 2:1–2). I understand our struggle to be with our default human nature—what is often called our sin nature (Romans 7:14–25).

This nature is at odds with the nature of God. We are self-focused and self-serving. God is self-emptying and self-giving. We are ego driven, living out of a what's-in-it-for-me spirit. God lives out of a servant spirit. We use power over, down against others for our own advantage. God uses power to serve, addressing the needs of the other and nurturing them into emotionally–relationally–spiritually maturity. We live out of merit-based thinking, relating to others based on what we think they deserve. God relates out of grace and forgiveness. We harbor hurts and hold grudges. God forgives ... freely, unconditionally, lavishly. We divide people into us–them groups, viewing the other as less than us. God embraces all as his beloved children. God never gives up on or abandons anyone ... including us! When our default, self-serving, power-over nature—"the spirit of disobedience" (Ephesians 2:2)—gets embodied in and institutionalized in the structures and systems of the world, then the world is hostile to the ways of God.

As for Satan and the cosmic powers and spiritual forces of evil, Satan was defeated in Jesus's death and resurrection.

His power has been broken. "The one who is in you (the Spirit) is greater than the one who is in the world" (1 John 4:4). Focusing on so-called spiritual warfare distracts us from learning and living the ways of God that Jesus taught. It keeps us living out of fear rather than an inner disposition of peace and joy and thanksgiving.

To stand firm in their new calling, the Ephesians needed to put on the full armor of God, including the sword of the Spirit. Every piece of the armor of God was designed to defend us from the attacks of this hostile world ... except the sword of the Spirit. It is the only offensive weapon in the armor. The armor of God—truth, righteousness, the gospel of peace, faith, salvation—empowers us to stand firm in the face of a world at odds with the ways of God. It allows us to deflect those things that come at us, seeking to weaken us and defeat us, squeezing us back into its mold. However, the sword of the Spirit is the one piece of the armor that we use to fight back. The sword is "the word of God" (Ephesians 6:17). Many people today use the phrase "the word of God" in reference to the Bible, but the biblical writer was not referring to the Bible. The word of God is what God says through his Son and through the Spirit. It is the spiritual truth the Spirit teaches us (1 Corinthians 2:6–16). Spiritual truth is the way we counter the false thinking and self-destructive ways of the world.

Spiritual truth—the renewing of the mind (Romans 12:2; Ephesians 4:23)—is what the Spirit uses to transform our hearts and minds. It is also the means by which the world will be transformed and a new heaven and earth created. It is what we use in bringing the kingdom into reality in our world.

Chapter 23

Christ Lives in Me

It is Christ who lives in me.

— Galatians 2:20

Through the indwelling Spirit, Christ lives in me. As I understand it, these two concepts in Paul's thought—"Christ lives in me" (Galatians 2:20) and "live by the Spirit" (Galatians 5:16)—speak of the same reality. In the first reference, Paul was speaking of his own personal experience. In the second, he applied his experience to all who are followers of Christ—to us.

When we are led by the Spirit (Galatians 5:18, 25), the Spirit leads us to live the kind of life Christ lived. Thus, as we keep in step with the Spirit (Galatians 5:25 NIV), we participate in Christ's life. As we live by the Spirit (Galatians 5:16), Christ lives in us and through us. Paul specifically links these two concepts together in his teaching about life in the Spirit in Romans 8. In verse 9, Paul wrote, "[Y]ou are in the Spirit since the Spirit of God dwells in you." In the next verse, he wrote "if Christ is in you" (Romans 8:10). The Spirit dwells in you; Christ is in you. Through the indwelling Spirit, Christ lives in us.

Paul's argument (Galatians 2:15–21) and instructions (Galatians 5:13–26) in his letter to the Galatians help us understand this Spirit-based way of living. This Spirit-based way of living is the flip side of being crucified with Christ. "I have been crucified with Christ; and it is no longer I who live, but it is Christ who lives in me" (Galatians 2:19b–20). It is the resurrection side of Christ's pattern of death and resurrection (Philippians 3:10–11). We, like Christ, die to our ego-based self with its self-serving nature (Matthew 16:24–26). The Spirit leads us to choose to follow Jesus and then empowers us to live out our decision. Through the power of the Spirit, we choose—over and over—to not live out of our default what's-in-it-for-me spirit. We die to this self-centered, self-serving nature so that we might live to God (Galatians 2:19).

This Spirit-based way of living moves us beyond the black-and-white, right-or-wrong thinking of the law (Galatians 2:19). The Spirit, not a set of rules or some cultural norm or religious standard of expectations, guides our life. We live out of a servant spirit, following the path of love (Galatians 5:13–14) and discerning the Spirit's guidance. Humility, grace, and forgiveness shape how we view and relate to others.

This Spirit-based way of living is living by faith. It is patterned after the kind of faith that Jesus had. "And the life I now live in the flesh I live by the faith *of* the Son of God" (Galatians 2:20, alternate reading, emphasis added). The idea is not so much that we have faith in Christ as the Son of God—"by faith in the Son of God" (Galatians 2:20). Rather, it is that we trust God the way Jesus trusted God. We build our lives on the settled belief that God is who Jesus revealed God to be—a God of self-giving love who relates to us out of who God is, not who we are; a compassionate and merciful God who relates to us with grace and forgiveness rather than with judgment and condemnation. We trust God to accept us as we are (justification, Galatians 2:21). We trust God to walk with us through whatever life brings our way, working in it to conform us to the image of the Son (Romans 8:28–29). We trust that God is committed to growing us up into emotional–relational–spiritual maturity that reflects the likeness of Christ. We trust that God's steadfast love will never waiver or falter. We trust that God's faithful love will never give up on us or abandon us. The Spirit nurtures this kind of faith in us so that we live with the confidence of a child of God who relates to God as "Abba, Father" (Romans 8:14–17; Galatians 4:6).

This Spirit-based way of living produces a transformed life. The Spirit leads us on a spiritual journey of inner transformation. As we keep in step with the Spirit's guidance, the Spirit grows us up emotionally–relationally–spiritually, engraining the character of Christ in the core of our being— the mystery the writer of Colossians identified as "Christ in you, the hope of glory" (Colossians 1:27).

This Spirit-based way of living is like a divine dance. The Spirit leads; we follow. We keep in step with the Spirit's guidance (Galatians 5:25 NIV). Thus, this Spirit-based way of living calls for intentionality from us. It calls us to cultivate the mind of Christ within us (1 Corinthians 2:16b). It calls us to cultivate a discernment of the Spirit in our lives. It calls us to cultivate self-awareness and self-management (Galatians 5:23) so that we can choose to follow the Spirit's lead. It involves the conscious choice to rely upon the Spirit's power as we seek to follow the Spirit's lead.

As we live by the Spirit, following the Spirit's lead and trusting the Spirit's power, Christ lives in us and through us. In addition, the character of Christ is engrained within us. The kind of life Christ lived becomes our life. Christ lives in us and through us.

Thanks be to God!

Chapter 24

God's Earnest Money

*You were marked with the seal of the promised
Holy Spirit; this is the pledge of our inheritance
toward redemption as God's own people.*

— Ephesians 1:13–14

In negotiating a contract to purchase a home, a buyer makes a down payment to the seller. The down payment is the buyer's pledge that he will fulfill the contract and purchase the home. This upfront money is evidence that the sale will be completed. It provides the seller assurance during the time it takes to finalize the transaction. In the real estate world, this upfront money is called earnest money.

In the letter to the Ephesians, the biblical writer spoke of the Spirit as God's pledge—the word in the original means "earnest money"—given to us regarding our redemption (Ephesians 1:14). The Spirit is God's down payment guaranteeing the completion of God's transforming work in our lives.[43]

The Spirit is God's mark on our lives, identifying us as God's children (Ephesians 1:13).[44] The Spirit's work in our lives—whether cleansing our guilt with forgiveness, giving us peace that quietens our anxiety, sustaining us in the face of suffering, granting insight into the ways of God, providing power to do what we cannot do in our own strength, or empowering us to love as Jesus loves—assures us that we are God's children. Such assurance stirs hope (Romans 5:5)—the hope of sharing God's glory, that is, God's character (Romans 5:2). The Spirit's work in our lives is concrete evidence that God is making good on God's promise to bring us to Christ-like maturity. The Spirit is God's pledge—earnest money—that God will not stop working until our salvation—the transformation of our heart and mind—is complete.

Such assurance and hope sustain us on our journey. In the midst of suffering, in the face of yet another failure, as we wrestle with that persistent, recurring sin, as we struggle with the frustrations of our still-in-process nature, the Spirit's presence in our lives assures us of God's faithful love that does not give up on us or abandon us. The Spirit's presence reminds us that God works to transform these challenges into greater strength and personal growth (Romans 5:2–5).

The Spirit is God's down payment—earnest money—assuring us that God will complete the transformation of our hearts and minds. The outcome of our salvation is certain. We will be like Jesus (1 John 3:2), measuring up to the full stature of Christ (Ephesians 4:13). With God's earnest money in our pocket, we press on (Philippians 3:12), confident in the ultimate outcome.

Chapter 25

The Body of Christ

---

*Now you are the body of Christ and
individually members of it.*

— 1 Corinthians 12:27

The Spirit works to make God's salvation—the transformation of our hearts and minds, conforming us to the image of Jesus—a reality in our lives. The Spirit helps us grow up emotionally–relationally–spiritually (Ephesians 4:13–15). The biblical word for this process of transformation is *sanctification* (2 Corinthians 3:18; Romans 6:22; 2 Thessalonians 2:13).

The ultimate and inevitable outcome of this transformation of our hearts and minds is the ability to love as Jesus loved. As we grow emotionally–relationally–spiritually, how we view and relate to others changes. In transforming us, the Spirit transforms how we live in relationship with one another. The result is spiritual community. The Spirit's work *in us* produces spiritual community *with others*. We call this spiritual community "the church." Paul spoke of it as the body of Christ (1 Corinthians 12:12–13).

Paul's metaphor of the body of Christ communicates two essential elements in genuine spiritual community: unity (one body) and diversity (many parts of the body). The theological term used to describe such community is unity in diversity expressed in community.

Unity in diversity describes the pattern of relationship found among the members of the Godhead—Father, Son, Spirit. Their oneness lies in their shared character of self-giving, servant love. How that love is lived out is different for each, shaped by the uniqueness of each. Each gives freely and generously of self to the other, for the other. In God's eternal redemptive purpose (Ephesians 1:3–14), each gives freely and generously of self to *us*.

When the church is a spiritual community, it reflects the life of the Godhead, the life for which we were created—unity in diversity.[45] Such spiritual communities are always Spirit-designed and Spirit-empowered. They are the product of the Spirit's work in us, through us, and among us. When the church is a spiritual community, it is "a holy temple … a dwelling place for God" (Ephesians 2:21–22). It is an in-the-flesh expression of God's ways—the ways of the kingdom. It offers the community in which it lives an alternative way of living in relationship.

Apart from the Spirit's transforming work, churches are seldom more than human-designed, human-created institutions. Rather than reflecting the life and community for which God created us, they duplicate the ways of the culture in which they live. They are homogeneous rather than diverse. They function out of sameness rather than oneness. As such, they are vulnerable to conflict and division because they do not know how to deal with the diversity that is an inherent part of life. Authentic spiritual community is the result of the Spirit's work.

Chapter 26

The Unity of the Spirit

*Making every effort to maintain the unity
of the Spirit in the bond of peace.*

— Ephesians 4:3

In transforming our hearts and minds into the likeness of Christ, the Spirit transforms how we live in relationship with one another, creating spiritual community, i.e., the church. Spiritual community is the product of the Spirit's work in us, through us, and among us.

One of the two dominant characteristics of Spirit-empowered spiritual community is unity—oneness that transcends and transforms differences. This oneness is centered in Christ Jesus.

> For just as the body is one and has many members and all the members of the body, though many, are one body, so it is with Christ. For in the one Spirit, we were all baptized into one body—Jews or Greeks, slaves or free— and we were all made to drink of one Spirit. (1 Corinthians 12:12–13)

Unity is produced by the Spirit. It is the result of living out of a self-giving, servant spirit that seeks the well-being of the other, i.e., love. The unity or oneness found in spiritual community is intended to reflect the unity and oneness of the Trinity—the Three in One. The oneness enjoyed by the Father, Son, and Spirit is grounded in a shared character. Each lives out of a character of self-giving, servant love. All that they do individually and collectively grows out of and is an expression of self-giving, servant love.

The unity experienced in spiritual community is a precursor to the unity that God is seeking to bring to all of creation (Ephesians 1:10; 3:7–12). In Christ, the animosity and dividing wall that separated Jew and Gentile have been broken down (Ephesians 2:14). People of all ethnicities and social groups are now "members of the household of God" (Ephesians 2:19). Their oneness in Christ creates "a holy temple ... a dwelling place for God" on earth (Ephesians 2:21–22). The spiritual community, bound together as one in Christ, becomes an in-the-flesh embodiment of God and convincing evidence of the beauty of the ways of God (Ephesians 3:10). Such unity is essential to God's eternal redemptive purpose (Ephesians 1:10). It is to be protected and maintained at all costs–"making every effort to maintain the unity of the Spirit in the bond of peace" (Ephesians 4:3). The unity experienced in spiritual community is a gift given by the Spirit that is to be recognized, treasured, and protected.

The key to maintaining the unity of the Spirit is the mind of Christ. It is living out of the servant spirit of Christ (Philippians 2:1–11). Conflict between two of its key leaders was disturbing the church at Philippi (Philippians 4:2). Paul wrote urging the two women "to be of the same mind in the Lord." They were to come to agreement by looking for that which reflected the Lord's purpose, not their own desires. They were to embrace the mind of Christ, relating out of humility, seeking the well-being of the other (Philippians

2:3–4). In addition to humility, the writer of Ephesians said gentleness, patience, and "putting up with" one another were needed to maintain the unity of the Spirit (Ephesians 4:2).

Conflict grows out of what Paul called "the flesh"—our anxiety-driven, ego-centered self (Galatians 5:19–21). In other words, it does not take any effort to experience conflict. It is a normal part of our human condition. In conflict, each person looks out for their own interests and desires with no thought of or concern for what underlies the other person's position. Each defends his own position while attacking the other and the other's position. Winning—"getting my way"—becomes the objective. Power is used against the other for our own personal benefit. Such functioning is the opposite of the servant spirit of Jesus. It does not know the mind of Christ.

Conflict in the church—an all-too-common experience—occurs when members act out of their default human nature rather than out of their relationship with Christ. It happens when members protect their manufactured, ego-centric selves rather than living out of their crucified-with-Christ selves. It happens when members function out of what's-in-it-for-me thinking rather than out of the mind of Christ. It happens when members demand their way, equating it with the will of God and thereby the only way.

The antidote to conflict in the church is personal spiritual growth—the transforming work of the Spirit. As the Spirit conforms our hearts and minds to the likeness of Christ, how we live in relationship with one another is transformed. Unity centered in Christ and expressed in self-giving love displaces the ego-centered conflict that is an inherent part of our human nature.

Unity is the product of the Spirit's work in our lives, but it requires our work as well.

Chapter 27

Neither Jew nor Greek

There is neither Jew or Greek,
there is no longer slave or free,
there is no longer male and female;
for all of you are one in Christ Jesus.

— Galatians 3:28

The Spirit works to create spiritual community that reflects the unity in diversity of the Godhead. By transforming our hearts and minds, the Spirit empowers us to love as Jesus loved. That love is reflected in how we live together in unity in spiritual community.

One of the indicators of spiritual community is how it transcends social differences. "In Christ Jesus, you are all children of God through faith. There is no longer Jew or Greek, there is no longer slave or free, there is no longer male and female; for all of you are one in Christ Jesus" (Galatians 3:26, 28). A spiritual community created by the Spirit moves beyond such social differences as ethnicity, social standing, economic standing, gender, and sexuality.

Diversity is God's creation. It is the pattern found in all of life. It provides beauty and variety all around us. As with every aspect of creation, diversity is also a characteristic of our human nature. We are all different, by God's design.

The common way we humans deal with our differences is through segregation. We think in terms of us–them—what is called tribal thinking. We divide ourselves based on how we are alike. We associate with those who are like us while avoiding those who are different from us. We exclude those who are not like us. This us–them, tribal thinking and relating is rooted in fear of the other. We are afraid of how they are different. We see their differences as a threat to us and our way. Unchecked, our fear of the other will lead us to seek to destroy them.

The Spirit leads us beyond such fear and the us–them, tribal thinking and relating it produces. The Spirit teaches us to view the differences as God's design and as a gift from God. Just as the different gifts are what allow the Body of Christ to function healthily, these social differences add variety and depth to the human experience.

These social differences do not go away in spiritual community. They still exist. Social differences are not ignored in spiritual community. Rather, they are transcended. We see beyond them to something greater than the differences. We are one in Christ. As the Apostle Paul said to the Galatians as they dealt with the issue of ethnic differences, we are "all children of God" (Galatians 3:26). Together, we are the body of Christ (1 Corinthians 12:12–13, 27). We are a "new humanity" (Ephesians 2:15), "a holy temple ... a dwelling place for God" (Ephesians 2:21–22). Living together in unity in diversity, we offer the world an alternative to us–them, tribal thinking with its fear-driven segregation, violence, and war.

Such spiritual community is the work of the Spirit. It is only possible as the Spirit transforms our hearts and minds, empowering us to love as Jesus loved.

Chapter 28

The Gifts of the Spirit

*To each is given the manifestation of
the Spirit for the common good.*

— 1 Corinthians 12:7

The first characteristic of Spirit-empowered spiritual community is unity. The second is diversity. Unity is experienced in the midst of diversity.

Diversity speaks of how we are different. The New Testament writers spoke of two expressions of diversity: (1) differences in abilities or gifts (1 Corinthians 12; Romans 12:3–8; Ephesians 4:7–16; 1 Peter 4:8–11)[46] and (2) differences in ethnicity and social standing (1 Corinthians 12:13; Galatians 3:27–28; Colossians 3:11). In spiritual communities, the Spirit transcends and transforms differences. Rather than being a hindrance to unity, Spirit-guided diversity contributes to the strength, health, and functioning of spiritual community, while oneness in Christ overcomes social differences (ethnicity and social standing).

Our default nature seeks oneness in sameness—everyone being alike, everyone in agreement, everyone believing the same things. Sameness is not the same thing as unity; nor does it produce unity. Ironically, sameness sets the stage for conflict.

Whenever someone in a sameness-based group dares to be different or to hold a different opinion, conflict is born. Unity is only possible in the midst of diversity.

In 1 Corinthians 12, Paul spoke about the diversity of gifts (abilities) in the church. He spoke of gifts as manifestations of the Spirit (1 Corinthians 12:7)—evidence of the Spirit working in the life of each individual. These gifts or abilities are given by the Spirit to each one in the body of Christ.[47] Though the gifts differ significantly, each is given by the Spirit. The purpose of the gifts is "the common good" (1 Corinthians 12:7)—to benefit the community, its life, and its work.

Paul spoke of the importance of these gifts by equating them to the different parts of the human body (1 Corinthians 12:12–27). Just as the different parts of the body are what allow the body to function healthily, the gifts are what enable the church as the body of Christ to function, doing the work of God. The gifts are interrelated and interdependent (1 Corinthians 12:14–31). Each part of the body or gift has something of value to contribute to the body's functioning. The loss of any gift leaves the body crippled, the community impoverished, and one another diminished.

To underscore the interrelated and interdependent nature of the gifts, Paul identified two attitudes that undermine the functioning of the body and the health of the community (1 Corinthians 12:14–26). The first attitude Paul identified was the attitude of insignificance (verses 15–16). When I live out of this attitude, I discount what I have to offer. This attitude is generally created and sustained as I compare myself to another, particularly to what the other can do but I can't. This kind of focus on what the other can do causes me to overlook and thereby discount what I can do. "If the foot would say, 'Because I am not a hand, I do not belong to the body,' that would not make it any less a part of the body" (1 Corinthians 12:15). The second attitude was the attitude of arrogance (verse 21). When I live out of an attitude of arrogance, I discount what the other has to offer. I live as though I do not need the other or what the other contributes to the body. I live as though I am self-sufficient, needing no one else. "The eye cannot say to the hand, 'I have no need of you,' nor again the head to the feet, 'I have no need of you'" (1 Corinthians 12:21). Both attitudes cripple the body and undermine its unity.

For the body to function in a healthy manner, two different attitudes are necessary. One is the attitude of confident humility. "Confident" means I know my gifts, my passions, and my experience. I know what I have to offer others. Confidence is the opposite of the attitude of insignificance. Humility recognizes that anything I have to offer was first given to me as a gift of grace by the Spirit. The gifts I have to offer do not make me better than others. Rather, they provide me something to offer others in love. Humility is the opposite of the attitude of arrogance. The second attitude that contributes to the life of the community and the health of the body is an attitude of mutual respect. This attitude recognizes and values the gifts the other has to offer. Confident humility and mutual respect are the pathway to grateful interdependence on one another. They allow us to give freely and gratefully receive.

Diversity is found in all of life. It is God's design and God's creation. It is God's gift, given to enrich life. Diversity is an essential part of spiritual community.[48]

Chapter 29

A Better Way

And I will show you a still more excellent way.

— 1 Corinthians 12:31

Unity in diversity is only possible when we love as Jesus loved. That's what Paul said in 1 Corinthians 13—the love chapter. In 1 Corinthians 12, Paul taught the vital role of spiritual gifts in the body of Christ. After summarizing his thoughts (1 Corinthians 12:27–31a), he said there was something more important than spiritual gifts. That something more was love—loving as Jesus loved. Spiritual gifts are hollow and empty unless they are used in love (1 Corinthians 13:1–3).

Spiritual gifts are a dimension of our personality, set free by the Spirit. Love is an expression of character, made possible by the transforming work of the Spirit. Love lies at the heart of God's character (1 John 4:8). Steadfast, faithful love is the governing dimension of the heart of God (Exodus 4:6–7). The Spirit is at work, transforming our hearts and minds, so that love becomes the defining quality of our character. The Spirit is recreating us in the image of God, in the likeness of Christ. The Spirit is developing a servant spirit within us.

Paul is clear that love is expressed in how we relate to others. Love—read "the Spirit"—moves us beyond us–them, better than–less than attitudes (1 Corinthians 13:4–7). As we grow spiritually—again, the work of the Spirit—we are set free from our ego-centric, what's-in-it-for-me nature. We are set free to use our gifts and abilities along with our passions to serve others.

Paul's teaching about spiritual gifts and about love was the foundation for his teaching about how the gift of speaking in tongues was being used—abused—in Corinth, causing strife and division. Paul called the Corinthians—and us—to "pursue love and strive for the spiritual gifts" (1 Corinthians 14:1). We are to actively pursue growing spiritually while seeking to use our gifts in ministry to others. Both are the work of the Spirit!

Chapter 30

The Spirit's Guidance

Being sent out by the Holy Spirit.

— Acts 13:4

In their wilderness journey, the people of Israel were led by the presence of God dwelling in the tabernacle. The presence of God, symbolized in a cloud by day and fire by night, guided them on each stage of their journey (Exodus 40:34–38). Their experience of God's guidance in the wilderness reflects the Spirit's guidance in our individual lives and in our spiritual communities.

In his teachings about life in the Spirit (Galatians 5:16–26), the Apostle Paul spoke of the Spirit's guidance in our lives as individuals. The Spirit guides us in living out the spiritual truths the Spirit taught us.[49] The Spirit's guidance requires a response from us. We are not passive players, moved along on a cosmic chess board. We are active partners who have a choice in the relationship. The Spirit's guidance calls for a choice on our part to follow that guidance. Our role is reflected in Paul's words: "If (literally: since) we live by the Spirit, let us also be guided by the Spirit" (Galatians 5:25). Having chosen to live by the Spirit rather than the law,[50] we cultivate an awareness to and openness to the Spirit's movement in our lives. As the

Spirit guides us, we follow. We seek to keep in step with the Spirit (Galatians 5:25 NIV).

The book of Acts reflects the Spirit's guidance to individuals. In Acts 8, the Spirit directed Philip in sharing the gospel with the Ethiopian eunuch (Acts 8:26–40). In Acts 9, the Spirit directed Ananias to go to Saul when he had been struck blind on the way to Damascus (Acts 9:10–19). The Spirit guided Peter to reexamine and move beyond his attitude toward Gentiles (Acts 10:1–48). The Spirit guided Barnabas to affirm and embrace the inclusion of Gentiles in the church at Antioch (Acts 11:19–24). Agabus predicted a famine under the guidance of the Spirit (Acts 11:28). He later warned Paul that he would be arrested in Jerusalem (Acts 21:10–11). The Spirit indicated to Paul that he would be imprisoned (Acts 20:22–23).

Just as the Spirit guides us as individuals, the Spirit also provides guidance to spiritual communities. Again, the book of Acts reflects this work of the Spirit. The Spirit led the church at Antioch to send Barnabas and Paul on their first missionary journey (Acts 13:1–3). The Spirit guided the entourage in their missionary endeavors (Acts 13:4; 16:6–7). The Spirit guided the deliberations of the Jerusalem council regarding the inclusion of Gentiles in the church (Acts 15:1–29; see verse 28). Under the Spirit's guidance, the disciples at Tyre warned Paul about going to Jerusalem (Acts 21:4).

A key to the Spirit's guidance is wisdom. The phrase "full of the Holy Spirit and of wisdom" was used to describe the first elected leaders of the church in Jerusalem (Acts 6:3). These men were selected to address a conflict in the early church. The underlying issue in the conflict was ethnicity and culture (Acts 6:1). Under the guidance of the Spirit, the men addressed the issue in a way that restored unity and expanded the witness of that early church (Acts 6:7).

Wisdom is a gift of the Spirit (1 Corinthians 12:8). It is the ability to apply spiritual truth to a specific situation. It is the ability to see the implications of a specific truth applied to the situation. While such wisdom generally comes through an individual, it is recognized and affirmed by the larger community. We see this pattern in how the early church dealt with the growing conflict. The apostles recommended a way for handling the potential conflict, and the congregation embraced their suggestion (Acts 6:1–6).

The Spirit guides spiritual communities in putting into practice the ways of the kingdom. The Spirit guides them in living out the implications of the gospel. By following the Spirit's guidance, the work and witness of the community is expanded. The kingdom is brought into reality in a specific locale.

"Since we live by the Spirit, let us also be guided by the Spirit" (Galatians 5:25).

Chapter 31

Beware of Pouring Cold
Water on the Spirit

Do not quench the Spirit.

— 1 Thessalonians 5:19

I don't remember the specifics of my childhood experience, but I remember the feeling—which speaks of the deep impact the experience must have had on me. I also remember the experience was not an isolated one. It happened more than once, although the specifics were different each time. Sadly, I fear my experience was not unique to me. My experience was an all-too-common childhood experience for many of my generation—especially those children who just couldn't sit still or who couldn't be quiet or whose minds were always jumping from one thought to the next or who were not naturally compliant rule followers who bent over backward to please.

The experience has been described as "having cold water poured on you." Cold water shocks you. It takes your breath, getting your attention and pulling you out of whatever you are doing. Too often, what we were doing as children was experiencing the joy of being alive—the unfettered freedom (read: lack of inhibition) of being a child, the excitement of engaging, the delight of discovering, the enthusiasm of creating, the fun that is the heart of playing. The cold water came in the form of another's—generally a parent's or some other adult's—response. Our joy, freedom, excitement, delight, enthusiasm (did you know the word *enthusiasm* is based on two Greek words meaning "God in us"?), and fun were met with criticism and reprimand. Perhaps we were being too loud, or we didn't raise our hands to be called on before speaking, or we were too active and rambunctious in the house. The adult's intent was to pull us out of what we were doing. It was to get us to stop what we were doing so our behavior conformed to the adult's expectations. Sadly, the impact went far beyond what we were doing. It quenched the spirit. It squelched the joy, displaced freedom with fear, dampened the excitement, extinguished the delight, took the air out of the enthusiasm, killed the fun. It was like pouring water on a fire, extinguishing it. It was death dealing and spirit breaking.

This kind of childhood experience is what comes to mind when I read Paul's admonition: "Do not quench the Spirit" (1 Thessalonians 5:19). What did Paul mean? Paul's exhortation comes in the midst of his final admonitions in his first letter to the Thessalonians: "[R]espect those who labor among you (i.e., your spiritual leaders) ... be at peace among yourselves ... admonish the idlers, encourage the faint hearted, help the weak, be patient with all of them ... do not repay evil for evil but always seek to do good ... rejoice always, pray without ceasing, give thanks in all circumstances ... do not despise the words of prophets ... abstain from every form of evil" (1 Thessalonians 5:12–22). These admonitions were instructions about how to live as the people of God, as the followers of Jesus. Notice how challenging these things were. Review the list, identifying which ones you do naturally or easily. The key to doing any of them was and is the Spirit.

The Spirit teaches us the ways of God that Jesus taught—the renewing of the mind (Romans 12:2). The Spirit guides us to put those ways into practice in the specifics of our lives (Galatians 5:25). The Spirit deals with those things within us—in our hearts—that keep us from living the ways of God. The Spirit provides the wisdom of "how to." The Spirit empowers us to live them. In short, the Spirit is the key to living the exhortations Paul made—which is why he, in the midst of the exhortations, added, "Do not quench the Spirit" (1 Thessalonians 5:19). Don't pour cold water on what the Spirit is doing in you.

Paul's exhortation raises the question "How do we quench the Spirit?" How do we pour cold water on what the Spirit is doing? We quench the Spirit whenever we resist what the Spirit is seeking to do in our lives ... whenever we resist the truth the Spirit is presenting to us ... whenever we refuse to follow the Spirit's nudging ... whenever we refuse to examine our thinking or what is in our hearts ... whenever we cling to old ways rather than follow the Spirit's leading ... whenever we live out of fear rather than the boldness of faith. We quench the Spirit whenever we say, "*No!*" to the Spirit's work in our lives.

A second question needs to be asked—what happens when we quench the Spirit? The image answers our question. Something is put out, but that "something" is *not* the Spirit. The Spirit does not quit working. God never gives up on us or abandons us. The "something" that is put out is something in us. Our resistance to the Spirit impacts our sensitivity to the Spirit, our awareness of the Spirit, our openness to the Spirit, our responsiveness to the Spirit, our willingness to respond to the Spirit's work. Bottom line: we miss out on the Spirit's transforming work in our lives. We fail to grow spiritually. We get stuck in a condition of spiritual immaturity (Hebrews 5:11–6:1).

Quenching the Spirit is not the full story. Quenching the Spirit does not just impact us. It impacts the heart of God.

The writer of Ephesians exhorted his readers: "And do not grieve the Holy Spirit of God" (Ephesians 4:30). This exhortation in Ephesians is part of the writer's teaching about putting off the old nature and putting on the new nature, patterned after the likeness of Christ (Ephesians 4:22–24). This transformation happens as we are "renewed in the spirit of your minds" (Ephesians 4:23)—that is, as the character of God and the ways of God begin to shape our thinking. The renewing of the spirit of our minds is the Spirit's work. This transformation leads to changes in our behavior. Five specific examples of this putting off old behavior, replacing it with Christ-shaped living, are given in Ephesians 4:25–32. This transformation of nature, expressed in a change in how we live, is the work of the Spirit. When we cling to old behaviors, habits, and patterns, we resist the Spirit's transforming work. We quench the Spirit. We grieve the Spirit.

Our resistance to the Spirit's work in our lives—quenching the Spirit—grieves the Spirit. It creates pain in the heart of God. God longs for us to grow up spiritually into the likeness of Christ (Ephesians 4:13–14). The Spirit works to bring us to that maturity. The Spirit works to transform our hearts and minds, conforming us to the image of Christ. Our resistance to that transforming work grieves the Spirit. It breaks the heart of God. It leaves us stuck in spiritual immaturity.

Do not quench the Spirit. Do not grieve the Holy Spirit of God.

Chapter 32

Life in the Spirit: An Overview

In this book, I have attempted to describe the work and ministry of the Spirit based upon references to the Spirit in the New Testament. This chapter provides a summary of the Spirit's work presented in the book.

- The Spirit works to make God's salvation—the transformation of our hearts and minds, conforming us to the image of Jesus—a reality in our lives.
- The Spirit draws us to God, leading us to open our lives to God—what John's gospel calls being born again, from above.
- The Spirit teaches us the ways of God that Jesus taught, leading us into deeper spiritual understanding of God and God's ways.
- The things of God that the Spirit teaches us nurture within us a freedom in our relationship with God— what Paul called the spirit of adoption. We learn to trust and rest in God's grace and forgiveness. We live with freedom from guilt, shame, and futile efforts to gain God's approval.
- The things of God that the Spirit teaches us produce a transformation in how we think—what Paul called

the renewing of our minds. We learn to think with the wisdom of God and the mind of Christ.

- The things of God that the Spirit teaches us confront the deeply engrained attitudes and spirit out of which we live. The attitudes and spirit out of which we live are dimensions of the interior realm—the heart. In calling us to deal with these attitudes and spirit, the Spirit is cleansing our hearts so that our hearts and minds are transformed by the Spirit's work.

- The Spirit moves us beyond the anxiety and fear, negativity and angst, which are a part of our default nature, empowering us to live out of a spirit of inner joy and peace.

- Through this transformation of our hearts and minds, the Spirit empowers us to love as Jesus loved and to love those Jesus loved.

- As the Spirit transforms our hearts and minds, empowering us to love as Jesus loved, how we view and treat others changes. We no longer view differences (diversity) as a threat. As we understand that we are all one in Christ, the Spirit empowers us to embrace one another as brothers and sisters. We are all beloved children of God.

- As the Spirit transforms our hearts and minds, empowering us to love as Jesus loved, we use our gifts, abilities, knowledge, life experiences, and material-financial resources on behalf of others. We live out of a servant spirit, seeking to make a difference in the life of another in the name of Jesus.

- The Spirit empowers us to live in unity within spiritual community as the body of Christ and the temple in which God dwells on earth.

- The Spirit empowers us to do what we cannot do in our own strength.

- The Spirit intercedes for us, particularly in the midst of pain and suffering.
- Through the Spirit's transforming work, we become a new creation. Christ lives in us and through us.
- The Spirit is God's guarantee—earnest money—that all of this will become a reality in our lives before God is through with us.
- Our role is to walk in the Spirit, keeping in step with the Spirit as the Spirit leads us.

Appendix A[51]

Summary of New Testament Teachings about Spiritual Gifts

1. Spiritual gifts are referenced in three letters traditionally attributed to the apostle Paul: Romans 12:3–8; 1 Corinthians 12–14; and Ephesians 4:11–16. In addition, the author of 1 Peter makes a reference to the use of spiritual gifts in 1 Peter 4:8–11. The most extensive treatment of spiritual gifts is found in 1 Corinthians 12–14, where Paul sought to address problems concerning how gifts were being misused in the church at Corinth.

2. The importance of spiritual gifts in the New Testament.

    The New Testament church was not a highly organized fellowship. The New Testament record reflects a slow development of structure. The highly developed structure and institutional nature of the church with which we are familiar did not develop until much later. The early churches were able to function effectively because of spiritual gifts. The gifts were Spirit-given (1 Corinthians 12:4) and Spirit-directed abilities among the followers of Jesus by which the needs of the body and of others were addressed. Gifts enabled every person to have a place in and a way to contribute to the life of the fellowship.

3. Every follower of Jesus was and is gifted by the Spirit for ministry (1 Corinthians 12:7, 11; Ephesians 4:7). No one is excluded. Most are gifted with a cluster of four to six gifts rather than a single gift. The cluster is composed of gifts that complement one another.

4. The purpose of the gifts is the good of the body—that is, the church (1 Corinthians 12:7). Through these God-given gifts, every believer has a means for meaningful, effective ministry in the church.

5. The result of the proper exercise of the gifts is spiritual and numerical growth within the church (Ephesians 4:16). Through the proper exercise of the gifts, the church functions as the body of Christ (1 Corinthians 12:12–13, 27).

6. The key to the proper exercise of spiritual gifts is the Christ-like character of self-giving, other-serving love (1 Corinthians 13). Such character is pursued through spiritual growth and is a mark of spiritual maturity.

7. The importance of the gifts today.

The proper exercise of the gifts by every follower of Jesus will produce spiritual health and numerical growth for the church. The exercise of one's gifts will involve the follower of Jesus in a meaningful, effective contribution to the life of the church. A meaningful ministry is one that is fulfilling and rewarding to the individual, invigorates rather than drains, is a joy rather than an obligation, and is a ministry rather than a task or job. An effective ministry is one that meets the needs of others, thereby contributing to the growth and health of the body.

Appendix B

New Testament Passages Listing Spiritual Gifts

Romans 12:3–8

For by the grace given to me, I say to everyone among you not to think of yourself more highly than you ought to think but to think with sober judgment, each according to the measure of faith that God has assigned. ⁴For as in one body we have many members and not all the members have the same function, ⁵so we, who are many, are one body in Christ, and individually, we are members one of another. ⁶We have gifts that differ according to the grace given to us: prophecy, in proportion to faith; ⁷ministry, in ministering; the teacher, in teaching; ⁸the exhorter, in exhortation; the giver, in generosity; the leader, in diligence; the compassionate, in cheerfulness.

Gifts listed: prophecy, ministry (service), teaching, exhortation, giving, leadership, compassion (mercy)

1 Corinthians 12:4–13

Now there are varieties of gifts but the same Spirit; ⁵and there are varieties of services but the same Lord; ⁶and there are varieties of activities, but it is the same God who activates all of them in everyone. ⁷To each is given the manifestation of the Spirit for the common good. [8]To one is given through the Spirit the utterance of wisdom and to another the utterance of knowledge according to the same Spirit, [9]to another faith by the same Spirit, to another gifts of healing by the one Spirit, [10]to another the working of miracles, to another prophecy, to another the discernment of spirits, to another various kinds of tongues, to another the interpretation of tongues. [11]All these are activated by one and the same Spirit, who allots to each one individually just as the Spirit chooses. [12]For just as the body is one and has many members and all the members of the body, though many, are one body, so it is with Christ. [13]For in the one Spirit we were all baptized into one body—Jews or Greeks, slaves or free—and we were all made to drink of one Spirit.

Gifts listed: wisdom, knowledge, faith, healing, miracles, prophecy, discernment, tongues, interpretation of tongues

1 Corinthians 12:27–31

Now you are the body of Christ and individually members of it. [28]And God has appointed in the church first apostles, second prophets, third teachers; then deeds of power, then gifts of healing, forms of assistance, forms of leadership, various kinds of tongues. [29]Are all apostles? Are all prophets? Are all teachers? Do all work miracles? [30]Do all possess gifts of healing? Do all speak in tongues? Do all interpret? [31]But strive for the greater gifts.

Gifts listed: apostles, prophets, teachers, deeds of power (miracles), healing, forms of assistance (helps), leadership (administration), tongues, interpretation of tongues

Ephesians 4:7–16

But each of us was given grace according to the measure of Christ's gift. [8]Therefore, it is said, "When he ascended on high, he made captivity itself a captive; he gave gifts to his people." [9](When it says, "He ascended," what does it mean but that he had also descended into the lower parts of the earth? [10]He who descended is the same one who ascended far above all the heavens so that he might fill all things.) [11]The gifts he gave were that some would be apostles, some prophets, some evangelists, some pastors and teachers, [12]to equip the saints for the work of ministry, for building up the body of Christ, [13]until all of us come to the unity of the faith and of the knowledge of the Son of God, to maturity, to the measure of the full stature of Christ. [14]We must no longer be children, tossed to and fro and blown about by every wind of doctrine, by people's trickery, by their craftiness in deceitful scheming. [15]But speaking the truth in love, we must grow up in every way into him who is the head, into Christ, [16]from whom the whole body, joined and knit together by every ligament with which it is equipped, as each part is working properly, promotes the body's growth in building itself up in love.

Gifts listed: apostles, prophets, evangelists, pastor-teachers

1 Peter 4:8–11

Above all, maintain constant love for one another, for love covers a multitude of sins. [9]Be hospitable to one another without complaining. [10]Like good stewards of the manifold grace of God, serve one another with whatever gift each of you has received. [11]Whoever speaks must do so as one speaking the very words of God; whoever serves must do so with the strength that God supplies so that God may be glorified in all things through Jesus Christ. To him belong the glory and the power forever and ever. Amen.

Gifts listed: hospitality, prophecy, service

Appendix C

Description of the Gifts[52]

A. Administration

The gift of administration involves the ability to guide a group in accomplishing its mission in an effective, organized manner by clarifying purpose, identifying goals, devising and implementing plans, and evaluating the results.

Text: 1 Corinthians 12:28

Examples: Acts 6:1–7

B. Apostle

In the New Testament, the role of an apostle was twofold: the ability to exercise leadership with spiritual authority in relation to a number of churches and the ability to "go forth" to proclaim the good news of Jesus cross-culturally. In today's context, apostleship can be understood as cross-cultural evangelism or missionary work.

Text: 1 Corinthians 12:28; Ephesians 4:11

Examples: Acts 13:1–3; 2 Corinthians 12:11–12; Ephesians 3:1–9

C. Discernment

The gift of discernment involves the ability to distinguish that which is of God and that which is not—good from evil, truth from partial truth, the genuine from the pretentious, that which is healthy from that which is destructive. Discernment can be exercised in relation to what is said, what is done, motives, and objectives.

Text: 1 Corinthians 12:10

Examples: Acts 5:1–11; Acts 18:24–26; 1 John 4:1–4

D. Evangelist

The gift of evangelism involves the ability to share the good news of God's love in Jesus with unbelievers so that they respond to that love, becoming committed followers of Christ and responsible members of the church. In the New Testament, the gift probably referred to cross-cultural sharing of the gospel, what today is known as missionary work.

Text: Ephesians 4:11

Examples: Acts 8:4–6, 26–40; 2 Timothy 4:5

E. Exhortation

The gift of exhortation involves the ability to encourage, counsel, comfort, and motivate others in their spiritual pilgrimage.

Text: Romans 12:8

Examples: Acts 4:32–37; 4:36–37; 11:19–24; 14:21–22; Hebrews 10:24–25

F. Faith

The gift of faith involves the ability to perceive God's leadership and the confidence to pursue God's direction when others in the body do not.

Text: 1 Corinthians 12:9

Examples: Acts 11:22–24; Hebrews 11

G. Giving

The gift of giving is the ability to contribute one's material resources with cheerful liberality.

Text: Romans 12:8

Examples: Acts 4:36–37; 2 Corinthians 8:1–7; 9:2–8

H. Healing

In the gift of healing, God's power is channeled through an individual to bring healing to another. Healing may be physical, emotional, relational, or spiritual.

Text: 1 Corinthians 12:9, 28

Examples: Acts 3:1–10; 5:12–16; 9:32–35

I. Help

The gift of help involves the ability to do practical things, meeting practical needs, in a supportive role, thereby freeing others for a more effective exercise of their gifts in ministry.

Text: 1 Corinthians 12:28

Examples: Acts 9:36; Romans 16:1–2

J. Hospitality

The gift of hospitality involves the ability to make people feel welcomed and at ease. It is expressed in the willingness to open oneself to and/or make one's home available to others for their comfort and well-being.

Text: 1 Peter 4:9

Examples: Acts 16:14–15; Romans 12:9–13, 16:23; Hebrews 13:1–2

K. Knowledge

The gift of knowledge involves the ability to discover, analyze, and apply facts in a way that produces key insight and understanding for the issue at hand.

Text: 1 Corinthians 12:8

Examples: 2 Corinthians 11:6; Colossians 2:2–3

L. Leadership

Those with the gift of leadership have the ability to influence others, providing direction and guidance in the pursuit of the group's purpose and goals.

Text: Romans 12:8

Examples: Acts 6:1–7; 15:6–12; 1 Timothy 5:17; Hebrews 13:17

M. Mercy

The gift of mercy involves the ability to feel empathy and compassion for those suffering and in need. That compassion is translated into cheerful deeds that address the need.

Text: Romans 12:8

Examples: Luke 10:33–35; Acts 16:33–34

N. Miracles

God works through the individual who has the gift of miracles to overcome difficulties, to accomplish extraordinary things for the benefit of the gospel and the church.

Text: 1 Corinthians 12:10, 28

Examples: Acts 9:36–38; 19:11–12; Romans 15:18–19

O. Pastor/Shepherd

Those with the gift of shepherding have the ability to assume responsibility for the spiritual nurture and development of other believers, either of individuals or of a group.

Text: Ephesians 4:11

Examples: 1 Timothy 3:1–7; 1 Peter 5:1–3

P.   Prophecy

Those with the gift of prophecy have the ability to speak publicly for God with boldness, proclaiming God's word for the present and declaring how God is at work in the world. Prophecy refers to forth-telling as opposed to foretelling.

Text: Romans 12:6; 1 Corinthians 12:10, 28; Ephesians 4:11; 1 Peter 4:11 (speaking)

Examples: Acts 13:1; 21:9–11; Romans 10:14–15; 1 Corinthians 14:1, 3

Q.   Service

Those with the gift of service have an ability to recognize, respond to, and quietly meet the needs of others.

Text: Romans 12:7

Examples: Acts 6:1–7; Galatians 6:2, 10; 2 Timothy 1:16–18; Titus 3:14

R.   Teaching

Those with the gift of teaching have the ability to communicate truth in a clear, understandable, relevant way so that others are encouraged and edified.

Text: 1 Corinthians 12:28; Ephesians 4:11

Examples: Acts 18:24–28; 29:20–21

S. Tongues

The gift of tongues appears in two forms in the New Testament. It first appears as the ability to speak God's word in a known language that one has never studied, as in Acts 2:1–13. It also involves the ability to speak in a language known only to the Spirit and understood only by individuals given the gift of interpretation. This second expression is often viewed as a prayer language.

Text: 1 Corinthians 12:10, 28

Examples: Acts 2:1–13; 10:44–46; 19:1–7; 1 Corinthians 14:13–19

T. Tongues Interpreted

The interpretation of tongues is the gift of understanding and interpreting for others the ecstatic language referred to as "tongues" or "unknown tongue."

Text: 1 Corinthians 12:10, 30

Examples: 1 Corinthians 14:13, 26–28

U. Wisdom

The one with the gift of wisdom has an ability to apply spiritual truth to a specific issue as well as the ability to guide others through the practical application of a spiritual truth.

Text: 1 Corinthians 12:8

Examples: Acts 6:3, 10; 1 Corinthians 2:1–13; James 1:5; 2 Peter 3:15

Endnotes

1. In contrast to this common pattern of overlooking the work of the Spirit, some individuals and churches have exalted the Spirit to a status that seemingly eclipses that of Jesus. These churches identify themselves as charismatic or Pentecostal or full gospel churches. They often focus on selective manifestations of the Spirit such as speaking in tongues, healings, deliverances, etc. These churches view speaking in tongues as evidence of the Spirit in one's life. Their focus on these selective—dare I say peripheral—manifestations of the Spirit often blinds them to the heart of the Spirit's work.

2. I intentionally use the traditional references to the three members of the Godhead: Father, Son, Spirit. A modern trend, in an attempt to use less patriarchal language, is to replace these traditional terms with Creator, Redeemer, and Sustainer. For me, the traditional references point to relationships, while these newer ways of referring to the Godhead point to roles or functions. As each member of the Godhead lives out of a character of steadfast, faithful love, the "role" each plays is to create and nurture relationship that produces maturity and wholeness in the life of the beloved.

3. All scripture quotations are from the New Revised Standard Version unless otherwise noted (© 1989 the Division of Christian Education of the National Council of the Churches of Christ in the United States of America; used by permission).

4. God's eternal redemptive purpose is the central theme in the book of Ephesians. God's purpose is to restore unity to all of creation under the lordship of Christ (Ephesians 1:10). In that purpose, each member of the Godhead plays a role (Ephesians 1:3–14). In addition, the church plays a central role, embodying the unity of the Godhead (Ephesians 2:11–22; 3:10). Our personal salvation grows out of and contributes to God's eternal redemptive purpose (Ephesians 2:1–10). The heart of our salvation is the transformation of our hearts and minds into the

likeness of Christ (Ephesians 4:13–16) as we put off the old self and put on a new self that is created in the likeness of God (Ephesians 4:17–24). This inner transformation occurs as we learn to think differently, with the mind of Christ (Ephesians 4:23; 1 Corinthians 2:16).

5. The majority of these meditations were first published as blogs on my website—pastorstevelangford.com—during the season after Pentecost in 2021.

6. The Apostle Paul spoke of this indwelling in his letter to the Romans: "But you are not in the flesh; you are in the Spirit since the Spirit of God dwells in you" (Romans 8:9).

7. "Called alongside" is the literal meaning of the Greek term used in John 14:16.

8. The Greek word translated as "another" (John 14:16) means one of the same kind.

9. In John's gospel, the term *glorified* was used as a reference to Jesus's death, resurrection, and ascension back to the Father.

10. Compare Luke 1:1–4 with Acts 1:1–5.

11. The English word *messiah* is a transliteration of the Hebrew adjective meaning "anointed." The messiah was the anointed one.

12. The Apostle Paul spoke of this aspect of the Spirit's work in his letter to the Corinthians. The Spirit is the one who understands the deep things of God (1 Corinthians 2:10–11) and who reveals them to us (1 Corinthians 2:10a, 12–14) so that our lives might be shaped by the wisdom of God (1 Corinthians 2:6–7).

13. The word Jesus used can mean both "again" and "from above"—born again, from above.

14. The Apostle Paul spoke of this life-giving work of the Spirit in his letter to the Corinthians. "For the letter (of the law) kills, but the Spirit gives life" (2 Corinthians 3:6).

15. See John 14:17, 23, where Jesus taught the disciples this truth.

16. This chapter was first published as a blog for Pentecost Sunday in 2021—May 23, 2021.

17. See Galatians 5:19–21, where Paul wrote about the works of the flesh.

18. This description of Paul's term "the flesh" comes from my book *The Fruit of the Spirit: The Path That Leads to Loving as Jesus Loved*. Each of my books is available through my website: pastorstevelangford.com.

19. This chapter was first published as a blog for the Sunday after Pentecost in 2021—Trinity Sunday, May 30, 2021.

20. The Holy Bible, New International Version® (NIV®). (© 1973, 1978, 1984, 2011 by Biblica, Inc.™ Used by permission. All rights reserved worldwide.)

21. I develop this understanding of love in my book *The Fruit of the Spirit: The Path That Leads to Loving as Jesus Loved.*

22. In Isaiah 11:2, the spirit of Lord is equated with thinking—wisdom, understanding, counsel, knowledge, and the fear of the Lord.

23. I intentionally link emotionally–relationally–spiritually together as progress in one arena translates into progress in the other two.

24. Humility comes from doing our own inner work, addressing our issues and the anger, bitterness, and resentment they produce.

25. See Hebrews 4:14–16, where the biblical writer speaks of coming boldly into the presence of God.

26. Paul spoke of this law-based way of living as "a yoke of slavery" (Galatians 5:1b). He called the Galatians to stand firm in their freedom in Christ, warning them about submitting again to this kind of slavery. His warning points to something within us that naturally gravitates to this merit-based, law-centered way of living. It appeals to our sense of self-reliance and independence. It gives us a sense of power, albeit a false sense of power. In his letter to the Corinthians, he wrote "for the letter (of the law) kills, but the Spirit gives life" (2 Corinthians 3:6).

27. Thinking with a different mind is the root meaning of the word commonly translated as "repent."

28. This description is based upon Colossians 3:12–17.

29. In 2 Thessalonians 2:13, Paul spoke of this transforming work of the Spirit as "sanctification by Spirit." In 2 Corinthians 3:3, Paul spoke of the Corinthian believers as "a letter of Christ, written ... with the Spirit of the living God, not on tablets of stone but on tablets of human hearts." Their inner transformation as the followers of Jesus was a letter of recommendation of Paul's ministry.

30. In his defense against his accusers, Stephen accused them of sabotaging or resisting the Holy Spirit. "You stiff-necked people, uncircumcised in heart and ears, you are forever opposing the Holy Spirit" (Acts 7:51). Stephen identified their unwillingness to learn as opposing the Holy Spirit's work. Such resistance created stubbornness ("stiff-necked people") and a growing inability to hear ("uncircumcised in heart and ears").

31. These questions reflect the seven markers in God's plumb line that I identify in my book *God's Plumb Line: Aligning Our Hearts with the Heart of God.*

32. The word *perfection* carries the idea of maturity.

33. This understanding of the fruit of the Spirit is developed in my book *The Fruit of the Spirit: The Path That Leads to Loving as Jesus Loved.*

34. This chapter is adapted from my book *The Fruit of the Spirit: The Path That Leads to Loving as Jesus Loved.*

35. The outpouring of the Spirit on us is symbolized in baptism by sprinkling. The sprinkling of water on our heads calls to mind the tongues of fire that anointed each of the disciples on Pentecost as the Spirit was poured out upon them.

36. The writer of Ephesians identified this power as the power that raised Jesus from the dead—the power of the resurrection. "So that you may know ... what is the immeasurable greatness of his power for us who believe, according to the working of his great power. God put this power to work in Christ when he raised him from the dead and seated him at his right hand in the heavenly places" (Ephesians 1:18–21). "I pray that ... he may grant that you may be strengthened with power through his Spirit" (Ephesians 3:16).

37. Notice that to be a witness is to share the difference God's grace has made in your life. The common understanding of being a witness is to tell someone how to go to heaven when they die.

38. See Acts 2:4, 4:8, 4:31; 7:55; 9:17; 13:9; 13:52.

39. See this pattern in Paul's story in Acts 22:3–21.

40. Leading us to pray is another expression of the Spirit's work of drawing us to God and into a relationship with God. See again Chapter 2: Born of the Spirit.

41. That's what it means to pray "in Jesus's name." We pray with the spirit of Jesus, in harmony with the will of God.

42. Suffering is the context of Paul's teaching about the Spirit's interceding for us—Romans 8:17–25.

43. In 2 Corinthians, Paul spoke of the Spirit as a guarantee—"who has given us the Spirit as a guarantee" (2 Corinthians 2:5). In his letter to the Romans, he spoke of the Spirit as "the first fruits" as we wait for the completion of God's redemptive work—"the redemption of our bodies" (Romans 8:23).

44. The Spirit is God's seal, marking us as children of God. The imagery the writer used was of a king's ring, stamped in the hot wax that sealed a communication, verifying it was from the king. The Spirit and the Spirit's work in our lives are God's verification that we are God's children.

45. Ephesians 4:1–16 reflects this concept of unity in diversity. Verses 1–6 address the unity of the Spirit; verses 7–16 speak of diversity.

46. See Appendix B.

47. I understand the gifts to be dimensions of one's deep personality that are released as we grow in Christ.

48. See Appendices A, B, and C.
49. See again Chapter 5: Keep in Step with the Spirit; Chapter 6: Led by the Spirit; and Chapter 18: Filled with the Spirit.
50. See again Chapter 4: Live by the Spirit.
51. The material presented in the appendices was first presented at the First United Methodist Church of Round Rock, Texas, in a workshop called "What Can I Do? A Gifts and Graces Workshop."
52. The gifts described here are the twenty-one gifts specifically mentioned in the passages found in Appendix B. The description reflects my understanding of the gift. The passage in which the gift is mentioned is noted. Examples from the New Testament are also given. Multiple tools are available to help you identify your cluster of gifts.

CPSIA information can be obtained
at www.ICGtesting.com
Printed in the USA
LVHW111416080522
718210LV00005B/124